Praise for Apr
How To Raise & Train Your Peppermint Shrimp

"It's a great little book. Its breezy, informal style makes it fun to read and it would be very helpful to anyone that wants to raise these guys."
— Martin Moe, author of *The Marine Aquarium Handbook*, and *The Marine Aquarium Reference: Systems and Invertebrates*

"A smashing book, fun to read, and a real inspiration to those people who want to try breeding their marine animals."
— *Today's Fishkeeper* magazine

"In spite of its partially comic title and tone... April Kirkendoll's slim volume is of real significance."
— *Advanced Aquarist* Online Magazine

"Even if you aren't planning to raise and/or train your own Peppermint shrimp, this book is an excellent read."
— *Saltwater Aquarium* Product Reviews

"A fun book to read, the author has managed to take a complex subject and made it simple and even entertaining to read. Hard to find book, but worth it!"
— *Aquatic Realm* Book Reviews

"A great book! The book has been written in such a fun manner that it would have been great to read even if I wasn't thinking of raising my own peppermints!"
— J. Beyer, a reader in Australia

Books by April Kirkendoll

How To Raise & Train Your Peppermint Shrimp: A Hobbyist's Guide To Raising Saltwater Aquarium Shrimp From Egg To Adult.

The End of Cancer: Seeking A New Understanding To Defeat The Enemy Within.

Coming in 2009:
The Last Stand: Scientifically-Based Home Remedies To Defy Cancer at the End of Life. (February 2009)

Help! Somebody Gave Me a Fish! A Crash Course in Setting Up and Maintaining a Freshwater Aquarium. (September 2009)

How To
Raise & Train
Your
Peppermint Shrimp

A Hobbyist's Guide To Raising Saltwater Aquarium Shrimp From Egg To Adult

April Kirkendoll

Lysmata Publishing   **Miami, Florida**

Published by Lysmata Publishing
7635 SW 56 Avenue #D
Miami, Florida 33143-5652
www.LysmataPublishing.com

ISBN-13: 978-0-9667784-4-1
Library of Congress Control Number: 2008910960

Illustrations by April Kirkendoll & Shirley Collar
Photography by Nick Kirkendoll
Printed in the United States of America

First printing, August 2001
Second printing April 2002
Third printing, March 2005
Fourth printing, **2nd Edition,** January 2009

Visit Lysmata Publishing online for news on forthcoming books, writing contests, author information, and more!
www.LysmataPublishing.com

To my mom and my hubby,
You encouraged me even when I failed.
You always made me feel like I succeeded
just for trying.

Acknowledgments

This book would have been much more disorganized and confusing if not for the help of several people. I would like to extend my gratitude to them:

Martin & Barbara Moe
Olga & John Wollinka
Dan & Jan Spotts of Miami-Aquaculture, Inc.
Nick Kirkendoll
Amie Hancey

Preface

"Whoa! Cool! They look like little aliens!"

A lot of the people looking at my display at the aquarium show glanced at the seemingly empty tank and moved on to the neighboring tank without reading the poster hanging below it. A few folks, perhaps noticing the dust specks in the water column, squinted through the glass, read the title of the poster (*Larval Shrimp*), humphed to themselves and moved on to the neighboring tank. One young boy, however, made my day. He read the poster, grabbed the magnifying glass that hung beside it and after maybe 10 milliseconds he started squealing about little aliens. His excited yells attracted the attention of not just his friends but also some of those people who'd moved on to the neighboring tanks without paying much attention to mine. They came back to see what they'd missed. Pretty soon there was a line to use the magnifying glass as the kid pointed out the dust specks in the water. I drifted over to help explain things — now that somebody seemed interested — and was soon besieged with too many questions to answer at once. This book is a result of that day.

I expected people to be vaguely curious about what baby shrimp look like, but I never expected so many questions like, *how can I do this at my house*? With dozens of questions bombarding me, I felt like I gave only half-answers. There was too much information to say with just a few sentences. But I think I may also have given incomplete answers because I found it really hard to believe that so many people were fascinated with raising shrimp. I mean, a kid saying it's cool to see aliens in a fish tank is one thing, but sane adults? Before that day I'd come to the conclusion that someone who raises shrimp as a hobby (me) is just danged weird. Could there really be other people who wanted to learn how to do this too?

Even later, when I gave a talk at a Florida Marine Aquarium Society meeting about breeding and raising the Peppermint shrimp, I still didn't believe that anybody would show up to listen to that sort of topic. But a lot of people did show up and they asked a load of questions. I had more time to answer them, yet there still seemed to be so many details that I forgot to say. So I decided to write it all down. Here it is, everything I've learned about raising the Peppermint shrimp, *Lysmata wurdemanni*.

By the way, this book is not for beginners. You should already know the basics of aquarium-keeping, since much of your success will depend upon good water quality. You don't have to have an expensive reef tank setup and you won't need high-tech filtration equipment in order to raise these shrimp, but if you don't already know how to keep the parents healthy, there's no way you'll keep the kids alive. I probably didn't need to mention that since most people who want to learn about raising shrimp have most likely already seen some hatching at home and would like to try keeping them alive instead of watching them get eaten by fish and corals. My intention with this book is to provide you with all the details you need to raise Peppermint shrimp. I'll tell you everything I've learned, and all the mistakes I've made (no, scratch that. If I wrote down all the mistakes I've made, it would take up about 7 volumes), so you'll be able to skip ahead to the practice-makes-perfect part.

Oh, and yes, there is a small section on training your shrimp. I had to include it because of the clever title I chose. You *can* train shrimp, but only if they live in an "invertebrates only" tank. An active community tank tends to make shrimp shy. Most fish like to eat any shrimp — yes, even "cleaner" shrimp — who are silly enough to dance upside-down on the water surface...

Preface to the new edition of this book:

The first edition pretty much covered all the basics of raising and training Peppermint shrimp, so, with only minor corrections or additions, this new edition is in many ways much the same as the original. However, this new edition includes a few major changes, such as a greatly expanded chapter on raising other shrimp species, plus a brand new chapter on some new larval rearing techniques I have been developing. Also, while I have left the original chapter on commercial rearing alone, I have added a new section at the end of that chapter. In it, I describe in more detail how a system could be developed for a small scale commercial system devoted to the aquaculture of *Lysmata* species. Such a system could perhaps be modified to suit other aquarium species as well, and I include ideas for such modifications.

Table of Contents

Continued next page

Table of Contents (con't)

Introduction

I have always been fascinated by sex. The sex lives of animals, I mean. It doesn't matter if we're talking about birds or frogs or fish or rhinos or any other beastie, I always eventually try to get them to breed in captivity. My motto is: if it don't breed, it ain't happy.

If an animal attempts to reproduce in captivity, I take it as a sign that it's both healthy and happy. If it's not healthy, it simply won't have the energy to go through the motions. And if it's not happy — meaning that the environment you've provided doesn't "feel quite right" — then it will be too uncomfortable or stressed to even think about sex.

Even if you supply your critters with the right foods and a good environment, many times you still have to provide further stimuli (romantic music, candlelight) to get 'em in the mood. And most times it helps to have the opposite sex. What makes each animal healthy and happy and puts them in the mood varies from creature to creature. That's part of the challenge. By the way, the artificial induction of spawning through the use of hormones or chemicals is, in my opinion, cheating.

So whenever someone tells me that something spawned in their home reef tank, I cheer. There was a time when simply keeping a fish *alive* in a saltwater aquarium was an accomplishment. Heck, even the term "reef tank" was unheard of 20 years ago. A living coral reef in your home! Wow. People have improved the hobby so much that now fish (and other life forms) are living long enough and feeling at-home enough to reproduce.

It was one of those serendipitous spawns that got me into raising Peppermint shrimp. After keeping saltwater aquariums for a few years, I unintentionally made the "home" just right for two Royal Grammas (*Gramma loreto*) in one of my tanks and they began building a nest and courting. I feverishly began studying the reproductive biology of Royal Grammas — and saltwater fish in general — until late one night I looked into the aquarium with a flashlight and discovered larvae! *(Hey! They look like little aliens!)* It turned out that the baby something-or-others were shrimp larvae, not Gramma larvae as I expected. I was soon so fascinated and determined to raise shrimp that I forgot all about the

Grammas. Shrimp were *way* more complicated. They are sort of like aliens in that they have a strange method (to we vertebrates) of growing and reproducing. At that time, there was very little information on raising shrimp, and most of that concerned the kind of shrimp you eat, which are different enough to make that information virtually useless. That was over 24 years ago. My, how time flies! There's a little more information available now — even specific information on Peppermint shrimp — but it's still a bit sketchy. I hope to add enough useful details here so that you can avoid some of the frustrations I ran into.

Raising shrimp became my full-time hobby and secretly I dreamed of making my first million dollars from my mother's garage with a relative of the Peppermint shrimp, the Flame shrimp *Lysmata debelius*, but no such luck. After describing the process of raising and training your Peppermint shrimp I'll add notes on two other species of *Lysmata*, in case you may be interested in working with those. And this new edition will also include notes on other species of shrimp as well.

Shrimp Biology 101

Even though I'm going to try to keep this book as simple as possible, I still might use a few terms that might be new or unusual to the average reader. So what follows is a quick crustacean biology course. Don't panic. This won't be hard. First, the vocabulary and a little anatomy:

Anatomy & Vocabulary:

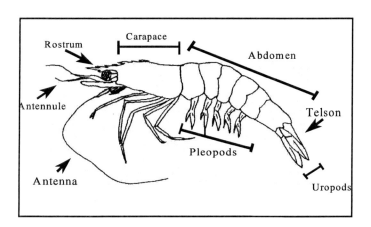

Antenna (plural antennae) = The long, whip-like structures on the head of the shrimp. Used for tactile investigation and occasionally as a kind of defense — flicking them at something to scare or push it away. Also, on cleaner shrimp species, the antennae are often white and serve as advertising banners for parasite-picking services.

Antennule = The smaller forked "antennae" in between the "real" antennae. Shrimp detect odors in the water with them. They "smell" with these things.

Rostrum = If you've ever been fishing using shrimp as bait, you know this as the pointy thing on top of the head between the eyes that stabs you in the thumb *every time*.

Carapace = This is the "head" of the shrimp. Actually it's a combination of the head and the "chest" fused together into one unit (the official term is cephalothorax. *Cephalos* = head, *thorax* = "chest"). Inside this unit, you'll find most of the organs of the shrimp. Since Peppermint shrimp are fairly translucent, you can feed them something bright-colored — like certain flake foods — and observe where the stomach is. The ovaries can be seen when they are filled with developing eggs.

Legs = Sometimes specially modified into claws or other appendages, but they're still technically legs. All crustaceans have 5 pairs of legs. They are members of the order Decapoda, which translates into "ten-legged". I mention this because of a game show question I heard once. They asked, how many legs does a Maine lobster have? And the "official" answer, which was argued about for a few moments, was "eight", since they didn't consider the claws to be legs. Which means, folks, that I would have lost that particular game show and all the money because I am educated.

> The tips of the walking legs have sensory hairs used for "tasting" whatever they happen to walk over.

Abdomen = Most restaurant-goers call it the "tail". They're wrong. This highly muscular region is used for emergency reverse propulsion. The true tail is attached to the very end of the abdomen and gives the shrimp traction during those emergency maneuvers. With one quick contraction of the abdomen, a shrimp can scoot backwards for a good distance. Since most predators expect a prey animal to move in the direction of its eyes (forward, usually), this surprise reverse move gives the yummy shrimp a decent chance of escape.

Tail = The fan at the very end of the abdomen. Without this fan at the end of the abdomen, the shrimp won't go very far backwards in an emergency. It's made up of the ***telson*** and ***uropods***.

Telson = The central spike of the tail fan.

Uropods = Part of the tail assembly. There are usually 2 of these "fins" on either side of the telson.

Pleopods = Often called swimmerettes. They are the soft, feathery-looking things underneath the abdomen. Used for forward swimming. Many kinds of shrimp glue their eggs onto their pleopods so they can guard and care for them during incubation.

What Makes Shrimp Different:

Shrimp live in little suits of armor. In fact, the word *crustacean* means crunchy critter (okay, so that's a loose translation). Their armor isn't as clunky as lobster or crab armor, but they have similar lifestyles and obstacles to overcome. A vertebrate (that's you) has an internal skeleton that is used for hanging muscles on. Without it we'd all be blobs on the ground, oozing from place to place. Our skeletons also protect our vital organs from damage. Crustaceans have exoskeletons — external skeletons used for the same purpose.

Nothing is perfect. The armor is pretty good protection from predators, but it has the drawback in that it doesn't grow — while the shrimp does. They have to shed their shells in order to grow and fix external injuries. That process is called molting. After building a soft, new exoskeleton underneath the old one, they secrete enzymes to dissolve the outer shell and make specific weak spots in it. Then they can crack open the old, tight-fitting shell — usually after dark — and squeeze out of it. I'm skipping a lot of details, but basically, it's a lot of work for a crustacean. By the time they've finished squeezing and pulling themselves out of their old exoskeleton, they're exhausted. Their muscles are rubbery, and the new exoskeleton is soft for a time. They're Superman on Kryptonite. Totally weak and helpless. Not only are they defenseless against predators, but they are also susceptible to any environmental stresses that they've been putting up with all this time too. That's one of the challenges of crustacean-keeping. They might seem fine in your aquarium for weeks, but when they molt, they're highly vulnerable to bad water quality, low oxygen levels, salinity changes, starvation, and more. It always comes as sort of a surprise. One day they're fine, the next day they're dead. When a fish is stressed or starving, you can see obvious symptoms. Its belly shrinks up, or its color fades or changes. Crustaceans look great until the day they die. That armor they live in hides their suffering.

Why is this important to know? Because the key to understanding the life of a crustacean is to remember that molting is a big deal in their lives. When they are not actively molting, they're getting ready for the next molt. Or recovering from the last one. That'll do for basic biology. The next section has an overview of general shrimp reproduction and then we'll move specifically into how to raise Peppermint shrimp.

A Quick Introduction To Shrimp Reproduction

So, how do they go about doing it? Another problem with having a suit of armor is that it also makes for some interesting challenges when it comes to having sex. Different crustaceans come up with other ways around the hard shell, but most can only breed when the lady is soft and weak. Peppermint shrimp are a bit casual about the term "lady". They are apparently hermaphrodites — meaning that they are both male and female at the same time. I say that from my own personal observations, but when I mention it to other biologists, they look doubtful. For many other marine species, hermaphroditism is commonplace, but for shrimp, it's pretty rare. There is another shrimp in the genus, *Lysmata seticaudata*, that has been proven to be a true protandrous hermaphrodite (starting out first as a male and later changing into female), but until some graduate student studies the reproductive biology of *Lysmata wurdemanni* (hint, hint), the information given here is just anecdotal.

Actually, based on my observations of three species, plus the information on that fourth one, I believe all, or at least most, of the genus *Lysmata* are hermaphroditic in one way or another. **[Update for Second Edition:** researchers have pretty much established that all of the shrimp in the genus *Lysmata* are hermaphrodites.]

So anyway, Peppermint shrimp mate soon after the "female" molts. While she is still soft and too weak to get away, the shrimp that's acting as the male (often "he" is carrying eggs) grabs her and swings underneath her crossways. The act of mating takes only a few seconds and is easy to miss if you're not paying close attention.

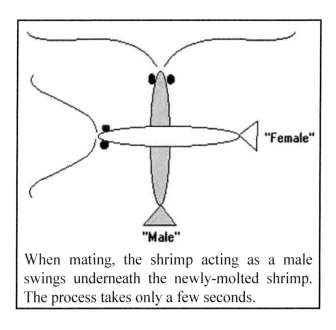

When mating, the shrimp acting as a male swings underneath the newly-molted shrimp. The process takes only a few seconds.

Almost all marine species from fish to snails to crustaceans produce eggs that hatch into a larval form that drifts about on the currents, eating tiny plankton, until one day it goes through a change called the metamorphosis — it settles down toward the bottom and changes into a miniature adult. Most people are familiar with butterflies, so I'll use them as an example. Butterflies lay eggs that hatch into caterpillars. The caterpillar is a larval butterfly and it looks nothing like the adult. After a while of munching and growing, the caterpillar forms a cocoon and goes through a metamorphosis into a butterfly. Shrimp have a life cycle that's similar to a butterfly's — without the cocoon — but the final metamorphosis from larva to postlarva (the miniature adult) can be just as dramatic.

Some kinds of shrimp produce gazillions of eggs and scatter them to the currents and hope that maybe one will grow up. Those eggs usually hatch into larvae that look little to nothing like the adults, and they are quite primitive, sometimes even hatching without important body parts like mouths!

Most other shrimp produce fewer eggs and instead of scattering them to the currents, they hold and guard them for a while, usually attached to their pleopods. The embryo can grow in the protected egg until a larger, more advanced larva hatches out, with (hopefully) a better chance of surviving to adulthood. Peppermint shrimp are more the latter type. They attach a few eggs, — anywhere from 100 to 600 eggs (yes, in the ocean that's just a few) — to their pleopods, and care for them diligently for about two weeks, cleaning them and fluttering their pleopods to aerate the mass. Then late one night, the entire egg mass hatches at once, the female molts a couple hours later, mates, and the process starts all over again. The larvae, which hatch with mouthparts and attitude, are on their own.

Shrimp larvae have exoskeletons just like their parents. They can't grow in a steady progression to adult form like human children do. Shrimp larvae grow in stages, through molting. They stay the same size for a couple of days and then, boom, overnight they can grow by up to 50%. The other fun thing is that each stage adds a body part: another pair of legs, stalked eyes, maybe some more mouthparts. And just like their parents, they can survive, everything looking fine, until the next stressful molt — and then you might discover that something's not right because you suddenly get high mortalities. I repeat, molting is a big deal in the life of a crustacean. The larvae have to "build up energy" in order to successfully molt to their next stage in life, which means that a starving larva won't have enough energy to survive a molt. Also, their aquatic world has to be fairly unpolluted so they don't have any external stresses to deal with as well. So, they need clean water and lots of good food. There it is, the secret formula for successful shrimp-raising, in one sentence.

The picture on page 14 is the Peppermint shrimp life cycle. It is not to scale. I made the larvae a little larger in that diagram so that you could see the differences from one molt to the next. I'll discuss the larvae in detail in another chapter. For now, here's the life cycle of a Peppermint shrimp, in one hundred words:

The adult shrimp produces eggs which hatch into the first larval stage. The larval shrimp drift around in the water column for five to eight weeks, molting and developing and growing. At the end of that time, they go through a metamorphosis and change from spidery-looking larvae designed for floating about the water column into something totally transparent, but recognizable as a shrimp. They settle down to the bottom to begin their new life. A few days later they gain the adult coloration. Twelve weeks after they hatch, they become sexually mature and the cycle starts all over again.

Peppermint Shrimp Life cycle

(Note: This diagram is not to scale. Egg and larvae have been enlarged to enhance characteristics).

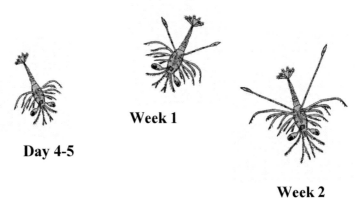

Week 1

Day 4-5

Week 2

Day 1

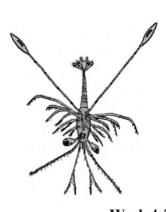

Egg

Week 4-5

Adult

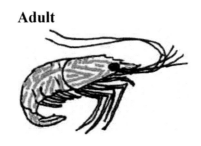

Breeding Peppermint Shrimp

From this point on, I'm talking specifically about the Peppermint shrimp. Most of the information I give here can be applied to other species in the genus, but the other species have variations on a theme and I'll address some of the differences for two other species near the end of the book.

Obtaining A "Pair"

There might be two species of shrimp that sell under the name of Peppermint shrimp. They look very similar. They both have transparent bodies with red stripes and longitudinal lines and look an overall pink color from a distance. The more obvious differences are that one is pinker, and bolder, and grows to a larger size (up to two inches in length). The larger ones produce pink eggs. The smaller ones rarely get longer than about an inch and a half and are more secretive (and thus are harder to train). They look pink until stressed and then they fade almost to transparency. They have dark, navy blue tails and they produce green eggs. If you look closer (I have. Yeah, I guess I need more of a social life), you can see differences in stripe patterns. They could be variants, I suppose, since in all other ways the two types of shrimp are virtually identical.

A more scientific way to determine speciation is to count spines. It's a great way to initiate graduate students to the joys of Biology. You count the spines, then use a key to determine what species you have (and then you have to fumble through decision-making statements like: does it have 4 supraorbital spines and 3 branchiostegial spines, or 3 of each? If you think that's difficult and time-consuming, just pause for a moment and pity the poor graduate student who had to do it first).

I had noticed differences in spination and curvature along the rostrum and did some quick research. The key I used to use to identify species went to North Carolina with a former employer, and so I haven't been able to look into the matter more thoroughly, but I determined that the smaller, paler Peppermint shrimp with the darker tails might possibly be *Lysmata rathbunae*, a species that's fairly common along the East coast of the United States. The other, pinker, Peppermint shrimp is probably the "true" Peppermint shrimp, *Lysmata wurdemanni*. It is mainly collected from the Caribbean and Gulf of Mexico.

Other than those differences, the two "types" of Peppermint shrimp are the same. They both seem to be hermaphroditic, although I have never witnessed the mating of the two kinds of Peppermint shrimp to each other. That may be more proof that they are separate species. The larvae of both types are identical in size, color, and behavior. Both kinds will pick parasites off your fish and eat those pesky *Aiptasia* anemones that plague reef tanks (although the *"rathbunae"* version eats only the smallest *Aiptasia* anemones, which helps to keep the population in check, but doesn't totally eliminate them). Neither species harms corals, although they will pick the diseased tissue off sick corals without bothering the healthy tissue. The traits of the larger Peppermint shrimp versions — being larger, bolder, and pinker — make them more suitable for the home aquarium since they "stand out" and get noticed which makes them better "pets".

Since I have never witnessed a mating between the two types of shrimp, and because a pair made of one of each kind never produces fertile eggs, I would suggest that you get a pair that looks alike. Size doesn't matter, just get two (or more) of the same variety. And that's the last time I'll mention the two types of Peppermint shrimp, since in every other way they are virtually identical.

Peppermint shrimp tend to be quite social, so you can get a crowd if you like. I've kept up to 54 in a 10 gallon tank, and the only thing you have to watch out for is starvation. If they're hungry, they *will* eat each other, usually by ganging up on the hapless victim after he molts. As long as they're well-fed, they'll group together quite happily under a favorite rock and sway back and forth like tiny Ray Charles impersonators.

By the way, I'm not saying that 54 shrimp in a 10 gallon tank is recommended, just that it is possible. I only did that little experiment because I had run out of tanks and temporarily housed the excess shrimp in the 10 gallon tank out of necessity. They survived the "experiment", but high population densities like that are very stressful. With two to six shrimp you can have a happy little colony that will produce bountiful numbers of larvae for you to kill... er, I mean, raise.

That just reminded me, there's a saying in the aquaculture field that in order to be a good aquaculturist, you have to kill a lot of fish (or shrimp or whatever other aquatic animal you want to place here). In that case, damn, I'm good. Over the years I've made a LOT of mistakes, some were really stupid ones, others quite novel. Raising Peppermint shrimp isn't simple. Again, I hope to give you a procedure with all the bugs worked out of it, but there still will be a kind of break-in period. There's a lot of "flick-of-the-wrist" stuff that is always necessary to learn and is nearly impossible to teach. So, a word of warning: you will kill larvae, probably a lot of larvae, before you get the hang of things.

The Spawning Tank

If you already have two or more shrimp successfully breeding in a community tank and you don't want to move them, fine. Skip to the section on larvae collection. This isn't a treatise on commercial shrimp farming, this is for the hobbyist who wants to try to raise a few shrimp for the fun of it. If you were trying to raise these shrimp commercially, then you'd want to save every last larva, not share them with your fish. When shrimp larvae hatch in a community tank, even when you are ready, you still only manage to get about 50% of the hatch. The other half disappears into joyous piscine orifices, filters, and anonymous nooks and crannies that become death traps. Since the Peppermint shrimp produce 100 to 600 eggs each time, 50% is still a fair number of larvae for the hobbyist to work with.

If you don't already have shrimp and you want to start from

scratch, I recommend giving your little pair or colony an aquarium to themselves. They'll be a lot braver without the busybody fish zipping about, eating most of the food (and larvae), and you'll be able to observe them better. I have successfully kept two to six breeding adults in a 10 gallon tank, but a better choice would be a 20 gallon or larger tank. The larger the aquarium, the slower the changes to the water in it. That means that it doesn't heat up or cool off as quickly as a smaller tank, a little evaporation doesn't change the salinity so drastically, more food can be added before it overcomes your filtration system — in short, larger tanks can handle a little more abuse. You can save your sweating for the larvae.

The spawning tank can be a simple setup: an undergravel filter and maybe an external power filter, plus the occasional water change will do fine. You need to place a lot of rocks to form caves and hidey-holes for the shrimp so they'll feel comfortable. They'll hide at first but later, when they realize that they're the only critters in the tank, they'll stay out in the open more often. Eventually they will learn that the human outside the tank might mean food's coming, so they'll hurry to the front glass in anticipation. I guess I should save this for the "Teaching Your Shrimp" chapter, but if you can get the shrimp to eat out of your hand, it makes observing their eggs a whole lot easier.

When you want to spawn other aquatic critters, you usually need to find out when they breed in the wild. That will help you to determine how long of a "day length" they should have and what temperature the water should be. For example, if a fish breeds only in the summertime, then that gives you an idea that you should keep the aquarium lights on for say, 16 hours, to mimic those long summer days. You would also adjust the aquarium water temperatures to those found in the wild during the summer. That fools them into thinking it's summertime.

Well, Peppermint shrimp breed all year around, winter, spring, summer and fall. You only have to provide them with a steady day/night cycle by using a timer — no turning the lights on and off at random times every day — and whatever's a comfortable room temperature for you is fine with them too. Just keep it stable as well. Don't allow variations in temperature from day to day or they'll stop producing eggs.

That may mean that you will need an aquarium heater to eliminate any day/night temperature variations. As they are a tropical species, it is best to keep your stabilized water temperatures somewhere between 78-82 F, but they will produce eggs even at a constant 70 F.

As long as you give your shrimp a stable, stress-free environment and feed them well, they will make babies without much more encouragement. When things are going well, *every one of them* will make babies.

Feeding The Prospective Parents

After you provide your shrimp with a good environment, you need to give them proper nutrition, in both quality and quantity. If you feed your shrimp only once per day, you may get some eggs, but the larvae that hatch from those few eggs will be weak and spindly, and not really worth the effort. You really should feed the adult shrimp at least twice per day, three times is better yet. The shrimp digestive system isn't terribly efficient, so several small meals are much better than one great big meal.

But even several meals of poor quality food won't give you Grade A eggs and healthy larvae. I like to give them a varied diet, as a kind of shotgun approach to providing all the vitamins and nutrients they require. I usually give them a good brand of pelleted or flake food in the morning, and save the frozen or fresh foods for later when I have more time to watch the shrimp eat. I make my own frozen food concoction for feeding my shrimp.

A friend of mine jokes around at restaurants, saying that the soup of the day is "Cream of Yesterday's Dinner". Well, my frozen shrimp food is a little similar. I don't really have a recipe. The ingredients change each time I make it. I just take whatever is available at the bait store — squid, shrimp, herring — and mix in something from the grocery store like clams or oysters, and I usually add a small amount of some vegetable matter like frozen spinach. Sometimes I'll put in some frozen krill or other food that I find at the local aquarium store (sometimes they have lobster and fish eggs. Yum!). I'll add a drop or two of liquid vitamin supplement and blend everything together. You should have your own special blender for this since the rest of your family will refuse to use it after you're done with it, no matter how much you wash it.

I pour/scoop the resulting green-gray glop into a plastic bag, squish it flat, seal it and throw it into the freezer. It's fairly easy to break off a small chunk of it and toss it into the aquarium. The shrimp will go mad over the gunk, and they'll take turns ripping at it. Or one will grab it and the others will chase it around the tank. Great fun! Be careful not to feed too much at any one time because it can pollute the tank very quickly. All those oils and proteins that make it smell so yummy to the shrimp tend to accumulate on the water surface if you feed too much at once. You could add a protein skimmer to keep things under control if you like, but as long as you don't overdo it, you really don't need it. Two to six shrimp don't eat that much, so easy does it. Besides, you'll be making frequent water changes as you'll find out later. Occasionally I'll offer my shrimp some live Brine shrimp, which is something else they seem to relish. Even after they're full, they continue to try to stuff more into their mouths.

This is sort of the "winging it" method of providing a good diet. If you're really interested in how nutrition affects the broodstock (the adults), eggs and larvae, a good book to read is Frank Hoff's *Conditioning, Spawning and Rearing of Fish With Emphasis on Marine Clownfish*. He goes into fair detail with the expertise of someone who tried to raise clownfish commercially. A hobbyist can make do with the "winging it" method, but if you're in business, you need to find specific ways to increase the numbers of high quality fish (or shrimp) you produce for your time spent.

And that's pretty much it. If you provide a good environment and good food often enough, not much else is needed. The shrimp will do the rest. Before long *all* the shrimp should have eggs in various stages of development.

The Eggs

This is just a quick comment on the egg development of Peppermint shrimp. When the eggs are first laid, they will be the color of the dominant yolk protein — either pink or green depending on the variety of Peppermint shrimp you have. As stated before, the "female" molts, mates, and then spends the rest of the day curling and uncurling her abdomen and fluttering her pleopods. By the end of the day you'll notice the new batch of eggs attached to those pleopods. Because the shrimp hides in the shadows of a little rock cave, it's nearly impossible to see the actual egg-laying. That flexing of her abdomen is the only evidence of egg-depositing activity.

If the eggs are infertile, or in any other way defective, they will drop off the parent shrimp in a day or two. That's pretty rare though. As long as you have a true pair and you are keeping them healthy and happy, you should have plenty of fertile eggs.

Depending on the water temperature the eggs will take ten days to two weeks to hatch. Warmer water temperatures increase the rate of embryo development, cooler temperatures decrease the rate of embryo development. If water temperatures get too hot, for instance, maybe your area experiences a heat wave, or perhaps your aquarium heater stuck on the "on" cycle without you noticing, then the apparently healthy eggs may drop off the gravid shrimp one or three at a time. I have only witnessed that when water temperatures exceed 83 F. It almost seems like the little strand of whatever material that glues the egg to the pleopod melts and lets go. Generally, your water temperature should be held somewhere between 78-82 F for proper egg development.

The parent shrimp will paddle "her" pleopods vigorously once in a while to aerate the egg mass, and she'll be seen picking through them with her pincers. She's either cleaning debris off of them or picking out dead ones, or possibly both.

During the incubation time, you'll see color changes take place within the eggs. They'll fade from their original bright pink or green to a kind of grayish color. About two nights before the actual hatching, the eggs will begin to get reflective. If you shine a flashlight beam on them that becomes more apparent. That reflectiveness is the individual eyes of the larval shrimp within the eggs.

Hatching always takes place at night, usually around 2:00 in the morning. Nighttime hatching decreases predation on the larvae in the wild. They have a chance to flow with the currents out to sea, away from the reef full of hungry fish. The larvae are attracted to light, which is handy for larvae collection, but out on a reef it's just another method of avoiding predators. If larvae drift up towards the moonlight, it gets them away from those hungry mouths on the reef that much faster.

On the night of hatching, the eggs will turn completely silver and the "female" will flutter them quite often. The expectant "mother" will be fidgety and may refuse to eat. The eggs swell with water so that the entire egg mass almost doubles in size. A few eggs may be seen hanging loosely and/or may drop off as the parent paddles the pleopods nervously. When the time for hatching begins, "mom" may just climb to the top of a rock and steadily fan her pleopods, sending little waves of larvae out in twos and threes. That method takes about 20 minutes to complete. Some shrimp, however, prefer to get it all over with in a moment. After climbing to the top of a rock and paddling her pleopods for a few seconds, "mom" will suddenly rise up and tail-scoot backwards all the way across the aquarium, releasing a huge cloud of larvae in her wake. Then she can relax and get right down to the business of eating her own babies.

Larvae Collection

Yes, you have to separate the larvae from the adult shrimp. Once the kids have hatched, they're on their own. "Mom" has no maternal instincts and will eat the larvae if she can. They become little swimming food particles after she's through with the business of hatching the eggs. The other shrimp will eagerly join in. If you have your adult shrimp in a community tank, the fish will wake up for a late night snack. Even if the fish and shrimp miss some, your filter will get the rest. Within just a few minutes after hatching, an hour at most, all those hopeful larvae will be dead if you don't do something about it. How's that for pressure?

So the larvae have to have a tank of their own. There are several ways to get them into their own aquarium. One way is to move the "mother" shrimp into the larval tank on the night of hatching. As soon as she has finished hatching all the eggs, you can move her back to the spawning tank with the other adult shrimp. That's all incredibly stressful to the "mother" shrimp (she *is* close to molting, remember), and sometimes she can die from the stress. She can also choose to abort the hatching and go ahead and molt, leaving the unhatched eggs on the abandoned exoskeleton. I've tried to artificially hatch those eggs, but the larvae never completely exit the shells. After reading several research papers on crabs, it seems that — in crabs at least — the female secretes a hormone that triggers hatching. Without this hormone, no hatching takes place. It may be that Peppermint shrimp have a similar hormonal trigger.

The least stressful method of course is to allow the larvae to hatch out in the spawning tank and then remove them somehow. That doesn't bother the adults too much, the larvae hatch out alive and wiggly, and all that's required is that the aquarist stay up all night long, periodically checking the spawning tank with a flashlight to see if hatching has begun. Then, when you are at your absolute sleepiest, the larvae hatch. I think they purposely wait until your eyes get sticky.

So then you have to focus your squinty eyes on the tiny dust specks wriggling around in the beam of the flashlight. You can balance the flashlight on top of the tank so that its light rays focus down from one spot and attract the larvae. They are highly phototropic (attracted to light) at this stage, so they eventually swim over and concentrate in the beam of light. Then, using a small siphon, you can gently slurp the little wrigglers into a cup or bucket and move them over to their new home. The trick, of course, is not to knock the flashlight into the tank while maneuvering your siphon hose around in its beam.

You know, it's a fun hobby and all, but this part of it can get really old, really fast. I cherish my sleep-time. So, borrowing from an idea I saw at an aquaculture trade show, I figured out a way to go ahead and sleep while my shrimp did their thing. The device at the aquaculture show was simply an air lift that moved water from one tank to another and back. But it got my mind to working on a gentle, automatic, larvae collecting device. [see diagram, pg 26]

My "Larvae Collector" consists of a plastic 2-liter cola bottle with the bottom and part of one side cut out. The opening on the side is covered with a fine mesh screen. The mesh of plastic or fiberglass window screen is too large. Plastic Weedblocker, available at many hardware stores or nurseries works well. Make sure you get the kind that doesn't have weed-killing chemicals imbedded into the plastic. You can also order fine mesh material from aquaculture supply houses, a few of which will be listed in the back of this book, as they are willing to do business with aquarists. You want something that has small enough holes to keep the larvae from going through, but large enough holes to allow a decent water flow. Using aquarium-grade silicone or hot glue, glue the screen into place. If plastic Weedblocker is your choice of screening material, then be sure to glue it so that the "bumpy" side is facing the aquarium and the smoother side of the fabric is on the inside of the Larvae Collector. As you will soon discover, shrimp larvae easily snag themselves on anything, and then die, so it's best to keep various stresses to a minimum.

Once your bottle has its screen glued in place, use ½ inch PVC pipe to make the arrangement as shown in the diagram. You don't have to glue any of the pipes if you don't want to. The only thing that's important is a layer of silicone around the part of the pipe that enters the mouth of the bottle. Shrimp larvae can find every tiny crack to wedge themselves into. If there is anything around that will snag, trap, or mangle shrimp larvae, they will find their way to it like little swimming magnets.

When an air line is pushed down the first tee-connector, it makes that first pipe into an airlift. Water and air from the main aquarium rises up the first pipe, the air escapes out the top and the water continues on down the next pipe and into the 2-liter bottle. You'll have to experiment with air flow. Too much air will create too strong of a current and the feeble larvae will flow up against the screen inside the bottle and get crushed by the suction. Too weak of an air flow and the larvae won't be dragged into the Collector in the first place.

The only thing missing from the diagram is a string tied between the tee-connectors at the "balance point" (the point on the Collector where you can hold it out level in the air with just one finger). After you build your Larvae Collector, you'll need to have a way to hang it in the aquarium so that it will stay at the appropriate depth in the water and not drift away. I tie a long enough string that will dangle over the edge of the aquarium and then tie a fishing sinker to the other end. After putting the Larvae Collector into the aquarium, you can let the sinker dangle outside, and gravity will hold everything in just the right place. You may have to experiment with sinker size, since your pipe arrangements may weigh more than mine.

Since Peppermint shrimp larvae are attracted to light at hatching, you can use a small, 15 watt (or less) night light outside the tank to attract them. There are now LED "moonlights" that work as well or better. Place the dim light just even with the opening at the bottom of the airlift tube. Then, late at night while you are sound asleep, your shrimp larvae will hatch, drift over toward the nightlight and get sucked into the 2-liter bottle where they will remain until you wake up the next morning.

This device can be used in most any tank, so if you have a reef tank with spawning animals and you don't want to disrupt your tank, just use this "Larvae Collector". Sometimes you can surprise yourself by setting it up even when you don't think things are spawning in your reef aquarium. You may end up with some unidentified larvae swirling around in your Larvae Collector.

One more note, on the night of a shrimp hatching, you should turn off or turn down the strongest circulation pumps. Shrimp larvae are poor swimmers and are easily overpowered by strong currents. Shrimp larvae are attracted to light, but if they can't *get* there, your Larvae Collector is useless.

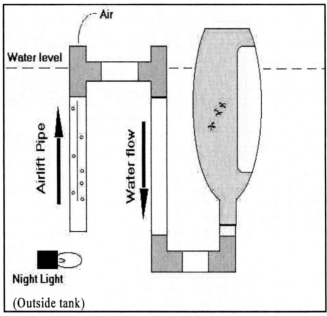

Larvae Collector made from plastic 2 liter soda bottle and ½" PVC pipes. See text for details.

Once your larvae have been collected, you will need to move them from the Collector to their separate larval rearing tank. The easiest method is to use a 3/16" air hose to siphon the little larvae to some transfer container, such as a large measuring cup or beaker. Moving the larvae from the Larvae Collector to the rearing tank will be discussed in the chapter titled, "Building The Nursery".

The Larvae

   I thought that this might be a good time to introduce you to your new wards, those little alien creatures that you've decided you want to try to raise. Before I do, this seems like as good a place as any to explain the measurements used in this book. As a citizen of the United States of America, I grew up using inches and feet and gallons for measuring things. Science uses the metric system. You may find me using both systems in this book, simply because my mathematical ineptitude produces a kind of mongrelization of the two. For lengths below one inch, I use the metric system because I hate fractions. If it's a choice between 1/25 of an inch or 1 millimeter (mm), I choose 1 mm. It's a whole number and easier to work with. But in the other direction, for things over one inch long I use the American Way because something like 61 centimeters (cm) means nothing to me, but two feet, well, I can easily picture how long that is. A 38 liter tank doesn't mean much to me either, but a 10 gallon tank, ah, that's very familiar. So I bounce back and forth between two systems of measurements. If this happened to be a scientific text, I'd have to stick to the metric system all the way through it. But it ain't, so nyah, nyah, nyah. For those of you to whom the metric system is just too incomprehensible, this might make it easier: 1 mm is about the thickness of a dime. 1 cm is about the thickness of a Compact Disc case (that's the *container* for the compact disk, y'all). Ten dimes stacked one on top of another almost equal the thickness of a CD case (10 mm = 1 cm). That's close enough for guesstimates, anyhow.
   Now back to our program. Here's the slightly more detailed

version of the Peppermint shrimp life history:

The adult shrimp produces eggs which hatch into the first larval stage known as a "zoea". All the more primitive larval stages passed while the embryo was still within the egg. The zoea looks vaguely shrimp-like. It's very strongly attracted to light at this stage, or at least, it should be. If it isn't, then its lack of energy comes from the parent shrimp's poor health or poor diet, and the pitiful thing probably won't live long, no matter how well you treat it. A healthy zoea is about two millimeters long and it swims in a head-down fashion, paddling its two pairs of legs furiously.

The zoea is fairly advanced as far as larval forms go, but pretty primitive by adult shrimp standards. Its eyes aren't on stalks, it doesn't have enough pairs of legs, and most of its other body parts are rudimentary. It does have a lot of spunk, though. It's very active and will try to grab anything that it bumps into. If it can hold onto it long enough, it'll give it a test-chew. If the object it has grabbed happens to be a sibling, it'll let go. Unless Peppermint shrimp larvae are starving, they won't eat their own kind. Even when newly-hatched larvae are put into a tank of four-week old larvae, they still don't eat each other, no matter that there is a huge size difference. If they are starving, however, they consider cannibalism an acceptable solution.

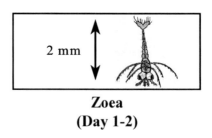

Zoea
(Day 1-2)

The zoea is greedy and will cling to objects much bigger than it is. In fact, Peppermint shrimp larvae are so attracted to larger objects that they will ignore tiny ones. So feeding first stage larvae something like rotifers, which is a common first food that marine aquarists give to larval fish, is a waste of time. The larvae can starve to death in a sea of food simply because they're looking for something bigger to grab. This is a big difference from fish larvae, which don't chew their food. Since they have to swallow their food whole, you have to supply them with tiny "bite-sized" items. Peppermint shrimp larvae come complete with mouthparts and some grabbing-legs to hold onto food and gnaw on it. The problem is, they are too small and weak to hold onto much. Most everything gets away from them. It's pretty frustrating to watch.

Newly-hatched Brine shrimp (see the chapter on Foods and Feeding) are ideal first food organisms. They are 1/4 the size of a Peppermint shrimp larva, they don't swim very well, and they come equipped with a packet of nutritious yolk — at least for a few hours, anyway. After several hours, the tiny Brine shrimp nauplii (really primitive larval forms of Brine shrimp) use up their yolk reserves and lose most of their nutritional value. Worse, they molt to *their* next stage, which means they get too big and active for your Peppermint shrimp. I'll describe that problem, and its solution, later. I'll also mention alternative foods.

The first week of their lives is a busy one for Peppermint shrimp larvae. With proper care and feeding, they will molt approximately every two days and get new accessories. They also grow a little with each molt. So around day 2 or 3, they get stalked eyes. On day 4 or 5, they get a pair of uropods added to their tails. By that time, they'll be about 3 mm long.

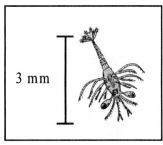

Larva (Day 4-5)

With the next molt, on day 6 or 7, they jump to around 5 mm in size and they get another pair of legs, complete with a new set of extra appendages that I call "spear-legs" because they are shaped vaguely like spears. They'll keep these strange appendages — they'll just get longer and longer — until metamorphosis and where they go to after that, who knows? One researcher guessed that they somehow move forward (they are part of the rearmost leg) and become the front claws, but I don't buy that. Those funky appendages seem to be designed for larval life only. I think they just drop off at the last molt, their purpose gone.

The spear-legs don't seem useful in any way, at least, not at first. Later on, around week 3 and beyond, they are apparently important in keeping the larvae oriented in that head down position. When one breaks off or gets bent around the other legs, the larva seems to have trouble figuring out which way is up, and does a lot of spinning. As the appendages become much longer and more paddle-like (they will eventually grow to almost twice the length of the body), they become important in steering through currents.

As an aside, watching the angle of the spear-legs can alert you to unhealthy behaviors, which can help you to head off disaster. Healthy larvae hold their spear-legs generally pointed toward their tails, or at least some angle between the horizontal position and their tails. Unhealthy or stressed larvae hold their spear-legs pointed more toward their heads (or some angle between the horizontal position and their heads). The stressed larvae may still eat and swim just fine, but the angle of their spear-legs is an early warning sign that you have some kind of water quality or disease issue developing.

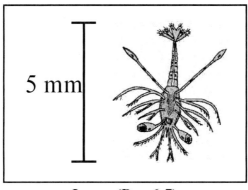

Larva (Day 6-7)

That molt to the fourth stage (the one where the "spear-legs" show up for the first time) seems to be a hard one for Peppermint shrimp. If you haven't killed off your larvae the day after they hatch, chances are you'll have plenty of survivors all week long. But the molt where they first get those "spear-legs" is one where you may lose plenty of larvae, if not all. If you can get past the first week, then you should have very little trouble for the next two to four weeks. It takes a minimum of five weeks to reach metamorphosis, although if things aren't quite right, they can stretch their larval life to eight weeks before they begin to die off one by one.

In all, from hatching to metamorphosis, there are seven major molt stages. "Major" molt stages means the ones where some noticeable alteration occurred, other than an increase in size. They continue to molt in between those "major" molts, but that's mostly for growth. It's only during that first week that you'll see the biggest, most obvious changes. The rest of the time will just be subtle things like growing bigger or getting more pairs of legs (after a certain number of pairs, you lose count and don't notice new ones) or making the parts they already have grow longer. So, they continue to molt around every two days, but after that first week, you may only notice subtle changes about once a week.

By the way, if you're really observing your larvae closely, you may try counting those wiggling legs and come to the conclusion that they have way too many. Adult Peppermint shrimp have five pairs of legs (and that includes the appendages with pincers, remember). Your larvae at one point can give you the illusion that they have eight or ten pairs, not including the "spear-legs". At least, that's what you see with the naked eye or with a magnifying glass. If you could take them and throw them under a microscope, you'd see that they really have the correct number of legs. The illusion is caused by the fact that each leg branches off into two parts, so that one leg looks at first glance to be two. If you want to add some more words to your vocabulary, they're called *biramous appendages*.

By the third week the larvae grow too large to eat newly-hatched Brine shrimp. Sure, they can still grab and stuff the tiny Brine shrimp into their mouths, but they spend more time looking like professional football players juggling a loose ball before fumbling it. They need larger food, the easiest of which is simply older Brine shrimp. I'll discuss feeding in another chapter.

By week 4, the larvae begin to look a little more like the shrimp they will become. Their bodies are nearly 1 cm in length — not including those "spear-legs" or their antennae, and they look pinkish from a distance. They have tiny pleopods which they can flutter from time to time, but they still use their legs as the main mode of locomotion. They can usually easily eat full-grown Brine shrimp by this time. They use their long, awkward-seeming "spear-legs" to herd the Brine shrimp toward their mouths. Since their "spear-legs" by this time have grown so much longer and more paddle-like, the larvae can use them as rudders to keep themselves from tumbling around in a current, which allows you to increase the air flow to your tank just a little bit. An increased air flow will help to circulate and increase the oxygen levels throughout the aquarium. But you don't want to increase the current too much, as the larvae are still quite fragile, especially when their antennae and other appendages are so long.

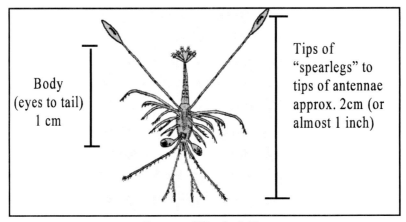

Larva (Week 4-5)
Tips of "spear legs" to tips of antennae approx. 2 cm (or almost 1 inch).

Around week 5, the larvae look pretty much the same as week 4 except they are stockier. If you measure from the tips of their antennae or antennules to the tips of their "spear-legs", they can measure close to one inch long. They look a lot more shrimp-like but they continue to swim with their spidery legs instead of with their pleopods, and they still have those long trailing "spear-legs". They'll spend much of their free time clinging to the sides or bottom of the aquarium, paddling their legs furiously like a helicopter about to lift off.

If you've fed your larvae well and kept them as healthy as possible, they should begin to settle to the bottom in ones and twos and metamorphose into postlarvae. At first, it may seem as though the larvae just disappear, but what really happens is that the newly settled postlarvae are totally transparent. All that's visible for the first day or two after they metamorphose is their white eyes. Two or three days after settlement they begin to get the adult coloration, and suddenly you discover tiny 1 cm long pink shrimp on the walls! After five to eight weeks of caring for the little guys, that's a happy sight.

The juvenile shrimp can be treated just like tiny adults. I usually leave them in the larvae tank for another week or so to give them some time to grow before I move them to another aquarium set up specifically for them. You can move them to an aquarium with an undergravel filter (where they will get lost among the gravel that seems the size of boulders) and feed them the same foods as the adults. Be careful of power filters, though. It would be a shame to have them get sucked into a filter after all that time you spent getting them to this age. Ask me how I know that.

About twelve to sixteen weeks after hatching, a mere seven to eleven weeks post-metamorphosis, they become sexually mature and can start making babies of their own.

Building The Nursery

Near shore habitats, with all sorts of decaying plants and animals and runoff from the land, have high amounts of nutrients in the water. Rough waters can stir up sediments from the bottom and suspend them in the water column. The salinity can fluctuate widely as a result of rainstorms or the lack of them. As you get farther away from shore, though, you find water that is fairly "clean" — relatively free of dissolved organics and debris, and salinity and temperatures, along with other water parameters, remain stable.

As I said before, most marine creatures have larval forms that flow out to sea and stay there for a time, drifting around in a thin soup made of microscopic plants and animals. The place that larvae call home is a sunlit, dark blue world with no walls or rocks to crash into, no choking sediments or debris to cling to their various spines and appendages, and few predators other than each other. Even though the waves may be huge, if you're just a dust speck, you don't notice them too much. It's just a slow up and down or circular motion to tiny planktonic organisms — unless it gets really rough, such as during a storm. But even then they have mechanisms to protect themselves. Sudden salinity changes, such as those that might occur when it rains, forces many larval creatures to sink deeper in the water column, which would help them get away from the turbulent surface.

That pelagic life is what they were designed for, so you need to duplicate their world in order to get your shrimp larvae to survive beyond one day. Obviously you shouldn't duplicate the hardships that larvae in the wild have to face. You should give them a world without predators, where the appropriate food items are easy to find, where all the days are sunny and calm, and life is easy. A larval Shangri-La. At least, that's the ideal.

They need clean water that's relatively debris-free, as they get tangled up in most anything. There needs to be a kind of "soup" for the larvae to drift around in, since they almost have to bump into their food in order to find it. And you need to have a gentle swirl to the water to aerate it and to distribute the larvae and their food evenly about the tank, but not such a strong current as to beat the weak swimming larvae against aquarium walls or each other.

You can set up a simple larvae tank on the day of hatching. A bare 20 gallon aquarium with an airstone in one corner and a single fluorescent light will do fine. High-tech, huh? Yes, you can design special systems for filtration and circulation for the larvae tank (and I have), but for the hobbyist, a bare 20 gallon tank is the least expensive and the least complicated way of doing things. There is maybe a little more work involved since you have to siphon debris off the bottom of the tank periodically and replace the water, but for one or two larvae tanks, that's not too much effort.

For this new edition, I have added another chapter concerning a slightly more complex larval rearing arrangement that works quite well... if properly set up and maintained. The information in this chapter, however, is much simpler and still applies for general larval care. If you have not yet attempted to raise shrimp larvae, it may be best to read and try this "bare tank" method first, before moving on to a more complex method of larval rearing. The bare tank method is still the simplest and easiest way to learn the basics.

A bare tank is necessary because it will reduce the number of objects for the shrimp larvae to run into and it will most resemble the environment they are designed for. As long as there is a gentle flow of water, they will slide along the walls of the aquarium rather than smash into them. If your current is too weak, then the oxygen levels will drop and that will cause problems too. It will take some experimenting to get just the right amount of circulation.

The size of the air bubbles matters too. Large air bubbles can break up the fragile larvae, especially as they get older and their appendages become more "spidery". You should get a fine bubble air diffuser for the corner of your larvae tank. If you place it in one corner, then the water will circulate the length of the aquarium, thus keeping the larvae from contacting objects for as long as possible. I've found that placing the airstone in the center of the tank beats the larvae up too much. They flow thumpity-bumpity up the curtain of air bubbles, then tumble into the nearest glass wall, slide down it to the bottom where they get a chance to "catch their breath", all the while slowly drifting back toward the curtain of rising air bubbles again. Even though you can still succeed in bringing a few hardy ones through to metamorphosis, I seem to get more survivors with the airstone-in-the-corner trick.

One more note on airstone situation before I move on: keep it suspended up off the bottom. If it's too close to the bottom, the larvae get stuck under it and die. Avoiding tight spots doesn't seem to be in their programming.

You should cover the sides of the larvae tank to prevent stray light from entering and attracting the larvae, which will mindlessly beat themselves against the glass for hours until they either exhaust themselves and die, or coat themselves with a layer of bacteria from the glass and die. A solid, preferably dark-colored background may make the food organisms stand out and help the larvae to find them a little easier. I prefer black or dark blue for the sides because that makes the larvae show up the best for my own personal viewing purposes.

Those of you who do not live in sunny Florida may require a heater in the aquarium to stabilize temperatures. Sudden temperature changes can kill larvae. But as long as temperature variations are very gradual, the larvae appear to have no problems. They merely slow their growth and feeding when aquarium temperatures cool. Delayed growth means a longer larval cycle. An aquarium heater adds stability to the temperature, which gives more constant growth and feeding. You will get the best growth rates if you set the thermostat for 78-82 F. The same note that I made about keeping the airstone away from the bottom or sides, to prevent larvae from becoming trapped, applies to the heater as well. The heater might be ideally located near the air flow anyway, to ensure good water exchange around it.

So, on the day of hatching you should have a clean 20 gallon tank with an airstone and fluorescent light ready to go. I usually keep it empty and dry until the time I actually move the larvae to their new home.

So, you now have your larvae tank prepared and last night your Peppermint shrimp spawned. Your homemade Larvae Collector is now full of tiny, white, swirling dust specks. Now you need to move those shrimp larvae to their new home. Attempting to move the entire Larvae Collector full of larvae will cause several things to occur:

1) The fragile larvae will suck up against the mesh as the water drains out the screens.

2) As you attempt to pour out the larvae into their new aquarium, they will not cooperate, and some will always remain in the bottle or piping, or they will get pressed onto the mesh by the escaping water.

3) Debris from the adult tank that collected on the mesh of the Larvae Collector during the night will also be transferred into the new tank along with the stressed and/or damaged larvae. Not a good way to start.

The best way to transfer the newly hatched larvae to their new home is to gently siphon them — using 3/16" air tubing — from the Larvae Collector to a beaker or some other container to wait while you drain the spawning tank of some water.

Move a few gallons of water from the spawning tank to the larvae tank. A "few" gallons is anywhere from 5 to 10 gallons. The reason I use the water that the larvae hatched in is because that way there are no sudden changes for them to deal with right away. The temperature and salinity is the same. They are *quite* sensitive to salinity and temperature changes. You can watch them die in minutes. Besides, it's a great way to add new saltwater to the parents' aquarium, thus keeping their water quality in good shape so they'll continue to produce lots of babies for you to practice with until you get it right.

I move the larvae into the beaker first because otherwise, as the water level in the spawning aquarium drops, the airlift device on the larvae collector stops functioning and some larvae can escape back into the main tank. Or, the whole (#$@%!) thing can turn over from the weight of the water in it and dump all of the larvae back into the tank. The shrimp larvae don't mind waiting in a small container for the 10 minutes or so that it takes to partially fill their new home. I run the spawning tank water through a coffee filter or some floss to remove any minute particles that I don't see while the water's in the adult aquarium, but which suddenly becomes quite noticeable on the bare floor of the kids' tank.

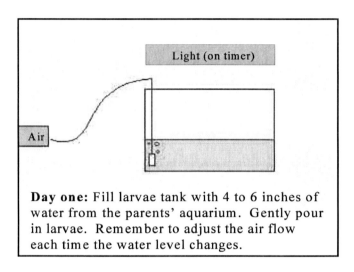

Day one: Fill larvae tank with 4 to 6 inches of water from the parents' aquarium. Gently pour in larvae. Remember to adjust the air flow each time the water level changes.

After filling the larvae tank with a couple of inches of water, you can gently pour the larvae into it. Go ahead and add the entire batch of larvae to one 20 gallon tank. I have tried numerous experiments on larval stocking densities and I've found that it doesn't really matter if you stock a tank with 100 shrimp larvae or 600 shrimp larvae, you still only get between 10% to 20% survivorship. One time I got 32% to survive, using this bare tank method, but apparently that was luck, not skill. For the record, if you get 20% to survive using the bare tank method, you're doing well. Usually the number is closer to 10%. In the new chapter addressing the addition of slow filtration to larval rearing tanks, I obtained greater than 60% survival on a regular basis, so it is apparently water quality stability, as well as abundant food, that makes for success.

Drop in the airstone and start the circulation. You'll start out with around 4 to 6 inches of water in the larvae tank on the first day and on each successive day you can add a gallon, slowly, so that there are no drastic changes to their environment as their aquarium is filled. Remember to adjust the air flow each time the water level changes. See the *Larval Care* chapter about what to do once the tank is filled.

People have asked me quite often about whether I use natural seawater or homemade (artificial) saltwater. I usually give the shortcut answer of "homemade" without really explaining why. So here goes. Originally, I used to use natural, unfiltered seawater for my larvae tanks, thinking that along with good, clean water, I'd also be adding plankton which could help feed my shrimp larvae. Well, yes, it added plankton to the tank. Some were harmless. More were lethal. I got plenty of microscopic predators that positively *thrived* in the Shangri-La that I'd painstakingly created for my shrimp larvae. The two worst offenders were medusae (itty bitty jellyfish), and a stinging hydroid that settled and grew on the sides of the aquarium (which may have produced the medusae). I once grew barnacles on the sides of the tank. I was so thrilled with them that I left them there to see what would happen. I never saw them eat any shrimp larvae. The food that I fed to the shrimp larvae, however, would disappear very quickly. Those barnacles would paddle those feathery sweepers of theirs as fast as they could, clearing huge swaths of aquatic territory. They could clean the entire tank of food particles in just under an hour.

Another problem with natural, unfiltered seawater is debris. Some people would call this a "no-duh", but there's a *lot* of sediment and other particles floating about in seemingly "clear" water. I never noticed that when I added the seawater to my community tanks or to the tanks that housed the adult shrimp. The filters most likely cleared out some of the debris, and the rest probably settled into the gravel, undetected. Well, okay, so I'm a slow learner. Eventually I got the idea to strain the water through floss or a coffee filter to remove the sediment and plankton. That solved a lot of the problems for a while. Then came two times when I killed off everything in the tank after making a simple water change that was supposed to *improve* the water quality. Even when you collect your seawater in a fairly clean area on an incoming tide, you occasionally get polluted water. Even small amounts of oil or diesel or insecticide from the overhead mosquito control plane is dangerous to invertebrate larvae, especially in an aquarium where the pollutant doesn't get diluted over time.

Anyway, I had more problems than I needed, so I switched to

homemade saltwater and I've never looked back. It's been fairly hassle-free ever since.

So, back to the larvae tank. After adding your newly-hatched shrimp larvae to the bare 20 gallon tank, you should feed them. They will begin feeding soon after they hatch if there's something available to eat. The problem is, that's usually around 2:00 AM. Lucky for you, Peppermint shrimp larvae can go several hours after hatching without food and still remain healthy enough to survive their entire larval life. The sooner you can move your larvae to their new tank and feed them, the stronger they will be. Don't wait any longer than 7 hours to feed them or else you'll get apparently healthy, active shrimp larvae that are destined to die in a day or three.

Let me try to clear that up. They can stay alive for up to two days without any food at all (after which, of course, they die). If you let them starve for 12 hours before you begin feeding them, they will survive maybe a few days and then die. Too long of a starvation period "adversely affects their life span" as they might say in scientific texts. But Peppermint shrimp larvae come equipped with enough energy reserves so they can "coast" from the time they hatch in the middle of the night until you wake up in the morning to move them to their new tank and feed them their first meal. You'll get the same results whether you wake up at 2:00 AM to feed them, or if you move and feed them a few hours later. It's your choice.

Larval Care

So you've managed to collect the larvae and put them into their own aquarium. You of course have the light on a timer so that the babies have some regularity to their day. You have covered the sides of the aquarium with some dark material to keep stray light from entering, and you have an airstone bubbling gently in the corner. All is well. So now what?

Well, for starters, you should feed them, but I think I'll describe the basic maintenance procedures first, and leave the details of feeding to the next chapter. For the first week or so, the only thing you should do to the tank, other than add food, is to trickle in a gallon of water per day until the tank is filled. I usually have several one gallon containers filled with newly-made saltwater just sitting around, ready to use. It's best to make up several gallons at once, perhaps in a clean garbage can, before dividing into individual one gallon containers. That way, all of your replacement water will be of identical salinity.

I set the water jug on top of the larvae aquarium and then, using 3/16" air line tubing as a siphon, I allow the saltwater to dribble into the larvae tank. Adding water slowly like that allows the old and new water to mix well, so that any salinity or temperature changes will be slight. Each new gallon you add dilutes the buildup of toxic metabolites (shrimp poop) and bacteria and keeps the water quality in decent shape during this highly stressful week of molting. Since the larvae will be molting and changing approximately every two days, the less you disturb them, the better.

Once the aquarium is filled, you can start the normal daily maintenance program. The larvae will spend between five and eight weeks in this tank (if you don't kill them off sooner), so this will become quite a habit. Shrimp larvae are highly sensitive to a buildup of ammonia and nitrites in the water, and, if you recall, this aquarium has no filtration. Initially, while there are no nitrifying bacteria colonizing the sides and bottom of the tank, that means that leftover food and dead larvae will quickly pollute the water. So for at least week two and three, you will have to perform a bottom cleaning daily, or at least every other day. This is loads of fun (which is my term for *tedious*).

First, you should create a "vacuum cleaner" for your larvae tank. You will need a piece of rigid 3/16" tubing that reaches all the way to the bottom of the aquarium, plus a little more to use as a handle. It's always best to keep sweaty, greasy hands out of the larvae tank whenever possible. (For a side experiment, if you want to see just how much stuff is on your hands, turn off the air and allow the water to become still. Look up at the surface of the water from below, then place your hand — or just a finger — into the water and watch the oil and sweat spread from it!)

Attach a length of 3/16" flexible air hose onto one end of the rigid pipe and, voilá, you have your high-tech, state of the art "vacuum cleaner". The hose should be long enough to dangle down into a bucket on the floor. My "vacuum cleaner" measures six feet. Two feet of that is the rigid tubing. So, you put the rigid pipe into the larvae tank, give a quick suck on the other end of the hose, drop the hose into the bucket when the water starts to flow down the tube (before you swallow some!) and that starts a siphon that you use to carefully "vacuum" the bottom of the tank.

While siphoning the debris into a small bucket, you have to watch out for living larvae that are near the rigid end of your siphon tube. This requires some head-standing and good eyesight (or at least a decent pair of glasses) to observe the working end of your vacuum cleaner and, whenever a larva comes near it, put a finger over the end of the hose in the bucket to stop the suction. Actually, come to think of it, I believe this is how I came to the idea of gradually filling the larvae tank during the first week instead of starting out with a full tank. Cleaning procedures are difficult enough when the larvae are big enough to see. When the larvae are small, as they are during that first week, you tend to suck up an awful lot of them.

The whole procedure doesn't take too long, maybe fifteen minutes at most, and then you can add newly-made saltwater to replace the water you removed (usually less than a gallon). Be sure to trickle in the new water the same way you did during the first week. While the new water is trickling into the larvae tank, you can examine the "dirty water" bucket and rescue any living victims of your sanitation. It never fails. There's always at least one helpless larva wiggling around down there, no matter how hard you try not to slurp them up. If it's swimming actively near the water surface, save it. If it looks weak, it might have been near the bottom because it was unhealthy and about to die anyway, and it might be better just to dump it.

It may be tempting to skip the daily housekeeping chore, especially if the bottom doesn't look that dirty, but diligence does count. It doesn't take long for things to get out of control in a filterless tank, and your shrimp larvae will use any excuse to die. No matter how small a pile it is, the larvae can get hung up in the debris and smother in it. Like I said before, larvae seem magnetically attracted to anything that is bad for them. Hmm, like most kids, I suppose.

But more seriously, it is the bacteria levels that are important. You need to keep the nutrients that the bacteria feed on under control. Even "good" bacteria can be dangerous if their population levels increase to the point of using up so much oxygen that the larvae either suffocate, or get stressed enough to weaken and become vulnerable to "bad" bacteria or other microbes in the tank. Ideally, the water should remain clear, but occasionally it may get cloudy. If the water turns a faint whitish color, it is probably a bacterial bloom. As long as the bloom is not excessive, and the larvae are swimming strongly, you don't have to worry too much about it. It should disappear in a day or two as the nitrifying bacteria settle onto the glass walls and adjust their population levels to the available "food" levels in the tank. When that happens, your life gets easier since the bacteria will help to detoxify the water.

After the third week, the walls of the larvae tank should become fully colonized by nitrifying bacteria and a thin coating of algae, which helps to purify the water in a limited way. The larvae are also a little stronger at that stage and are not *so* prone to smothering in debris. You no longer have to keep the place so tidy. Instead of daily bottom cleanings, you can switch to weekly cleanings, unless you are seriously overfeeding.

If the water turns cloudy from a bacterial bloom and stays that way, or gets worse, or if the larvae appear to be struggling to swim, that's trouble. You should probably make a larger than normal water change along with a thorough bottom cleaning. If that doesn't clear the water up, and the larvae are still struggling, and you are willing to take some time to save them, then they have to get into a new, clean tank, quickly. If you have another 20 gallon tank sitting around, great. Just fill it with new water, making sure, of course, that there's not too much of a salinity difference and the temperature is the same, and then transfer the larvae into it. If you don't have a spare 20 gallon aquarium available, that's okay. You just do the same procedures (described in a moment) to collect the larvae and place them into a small container to wait until you've drained, cleaned and refilled their original aquarium. If you're going to go through all the trouble of moving the larvae and draining the tank, go ahead and be thorough about it. Sterilize the tank by washing it with a weak solution of bleach and then rinse it well to get rid of any residue. Fill the cleaned tank with new saltwater. You can then pour the larvae into the cleaned tank and feed them again.

The procedure for moving the larvae is a bit tedious. You really don't want to take too much of their contaminated water with them, so you have to transfer the larvae one-by-one with just a minimum of water.

If they are less than 2 weeks old, you can use 3/16" rigid tubing to move them. You put your finger over one end of the tube while it is out of the water, point it at a larva, remove your finger and, *slurp*, the larvae shoots into the tube. Put your finger back over the end of the tube and the larva, plus a tiny amount of tank water will stay in the tube. Hold the tube over your transfer container or the other tank and remove your finger again to release the larva. Did I mention that this was tedious?

If the larvae are older than three weeks, you can use 1/4" tubing. When they are four weeks old or older, you can use a soft, fine mesh net. Just don't keep them out of the water for long. Move them quickly to the new tank or container— and be *careful!* They are fragile. Don't let them get tangled up in the net.

If you are moving your larvae to a transfer container to wait while you sterilize and refill their old aquarium, then be sure not to crowd them too much. Perhaps you will need more than one transfer/waiting chamber. Too many larvae in a confined space for a prolonged period of time will deplete the oxygen, among other potential problems, and you don't want to lose them after all this effort.

And that's pretty much it as far as maintenance is concerned. Don't be lazy. Keep the tank clean, and don't be shy about water changes. The only thing left is to tell you how to feed the little buggers.

Foods & Feeding

I sure hope you're reading this before you actually have hungry larvae to feed because one of the first things I'm going to describe is how to hatch Brine shrimp (a process that takes 16-24 hours). Brine shrimp *(Artemia salina)* is a wonderful, convenient food supply that is (or rather, can be) nutritionally adequate for all stages of the Peppermint shrimp life cycle. That's why I'm going to describe it first. After that, I will explain some problems with Brine shrimp and then tell you about some alternative foods. You can raise Peppermint shrimp larvae, with equal numbers of survivors, all the way through to metamorphosis on either feeding method (or a combination of both). You'll have to decide for yourself which method (or both) you'd rather use.

 BRINE SHRIMP

Brine shrimp "eggs" are available at most aquarium stores. Technically they're not eggs, they're cysts, which are Brine shrimp embryos in a state of suspended animation. Brine shrimp live in salty, inland lakes or ponds (thus the name *Brine* shrimp). About 90% of the *world's* supply of Brine shrimp cysts comes from the Great Salt Lake in Utah. During the rainy season when salinity levels drop and algae blooms and life becomes easy, Brine shrimp produce live young. When the rains stop and the lakes get saltier, they start to wrap their embryos in a hard covering so that the next generation will survive until the next rainy season when life is good again. The cysts float in the briny water until the wind blows them ashore. There they dry in the sun and wait for the rain to signal that it's time to hatch.

Those floating cysts are spotted by airplane and intercepted offshore by boats with collecting booms or they are scooped up by front-end loaders on shore and then they are cleaned and packaged into cans with the label *Brine Shrimp Eggs*. So Nature has provided a convenient, hatch-on-demand food supply just for the aquarium and aquaculture industries.

There are some problems lately with Brine shrimp "eggs" that I'll discuss in the section on alternative foods. For now anyway, newly-hatched Brine shrimp are really quite handy. You can keep a can on the shelf, or better yet, the refrigerator, until you need food for your larvae. Then, in 24 hours or less, you can have a perfect-sized, nutritious, slow-swimming, fairly non-polluting food item to put into your larvae tank. You don't have to keep a culture of something going all the time in order to have food for those occasional surprise shrimp hatches.

Hatching Brine Shrimp

I used a converted bathroom as my "Larval Food Culture Room". The "Artemia hatching area" is the shower curtain rod. From it, I hang bottomless 2-liter plastic cola bottles upside-down [See diagram, page 51]. Actually, *any* container will do for hatching Brine shrimp eggs. All you need is a container of saltwater and an air supply, but in order to get a better hatching, the eggs need to circulate well. In some containers, the eggs may eddy around in one corner and may not hatch, while the ones that swirl around in the water will. Many aquarium stores and aquaculture supply houses sell special Brine shrimp hatcheries that are inverted cones or pyramids that efficiently keep the eggs in suspension. I've found that 2-liter bottles standing on their heads do the same thing and they are a heckuva lot cheaper.

I hang the bottles by drilling two holes near the edge of the opening in the bottom. I tie a piece of string to each hole and tie an S-hook to the opposite end of the string. Then I loop the two strings over the shower curtain rod and snag the S-hooks back into the holes in the "bottom" (now the top) of the bottle.

On the other end, I drill a hole in the bottle cap that will allow me to slip a 2 inch section of rigid 3/16" tubing about halfway into it. I silicone or hot glue the rigid tubing in place so that the thing won't leak, then I attach a length of flexible 3/16" air tubing to it, which then loops up to the gang valve that's connected to the air pump located on top of the medicine cabinet.

There's two reasons for this arrangement. One is that the air comes up from the bottom (the neck) of the bottle, which keeps the eggs in suspension without any obstructions inside the bottle. The other, more important reason, comes after the eggs hatch. You need to separate the newly-hatched Brine shrimp from the eggshells. Luckily the empty (hatched) eggshells float, which gets them up away from the bottle cap. Unhatched eggs sink and settle right down into the bottle cap, below the tip of the rigid tubing siliconed or glued into it. The newly-hatched Brine shrimp feebly dance around in-between, concentrating in the area just above the neck of the bottle.

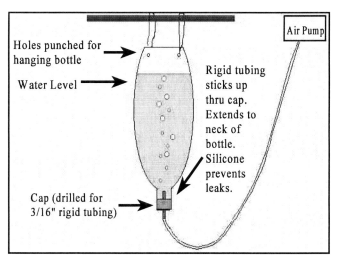

Homemade Brine Shrimp Hatchery
(2-liter bottle)

One teaspoon of Brine shrimp eggs makes enough food for one or two 20 gallon larvae tanks, with leftovers (which you'll move to another container later). I usually let the dry eggs float on the water surface for 15 minutes or so before I start the aeration so that they can absorb a little water and sink, otherwise, a lot of eggs float ever higher with the bubbles until you get a brown line of eggs well above the waterline which will never hatch. After that initial soaking period, start up the bubbles. You want a good current in there to keep the eggs swirling around, so don't be shy.

After the eggs hatch (which may be from 16 to 24 hours later), turn off the air and let everything settle down in your container. After about 15 minutes the empty eggshells will have floated up to the surface, the unhatched eggs will have dropped down to the very bottom and the newly-hatched Brine shrimp should be vibrating around near the neck of the bottle. For those of you with poor eyesight, the brown stuff is eggshells, the orange stuff is living Brine shrimp nauplii. [See diagram, bottom of page]

Once everything has separated, very carefully "unplug" the air line tubing from the gang valve without shaking the bottle and mixing everything back together again. Then lower the tubing below the level of the bottle and drain the newly-hatched Brine shrimp into a Brine shrimp net (you *do* have one, right? They're available at most aquarium stores). If you haven't duplicated my "Artemia hatching bottles" and you're using some other container instead, that's fine. You'll still need to turn off the air bubbles and let everything settle for a few minutes.

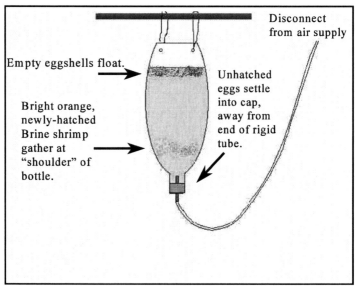

Separating Brine Shrimp From Eggshells

The only difference is that you'll have to siphon off the Brine shrimp nauplii into the net instead of simply draining them into the net. Rinse the Brine shrimp with freshwater to get rid of glycerins and other hatching-related oogies. *Never add the hatching water to your larvae tank.*

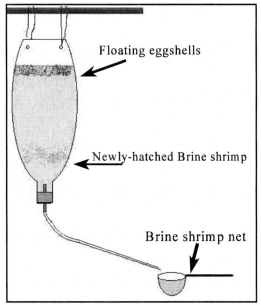

Collecting The Newly-hatched Brine Shrimp

Once you have used up the Brine shrimp, take the bottle down and wash it thoroughly before starting over, to get rid of eggshells and the thin coating of slimy substance that builds up on the sides of the bottle. About every third hatching, sterilize the bottle by bubbling a dilute bleach solution for about an hour. Rinse it thoroughly afterward. If your larvae seem to be affected by disease or some mystery ailment, sterilize the Brine shrimp hatching containers more often to eliminate possible disease introduction from this area.

Feeding Peppermint Shrimp Larvae (Part A)

A dime-sized drop of concentrated baby Brine shrimp is probably more than enough food for one *completely filled* 20 gallon larval tank. Be careful not to add too many Brine shrimp during the first two days when the water levels in the larvae tank are low. It takes fewer Brine shrimp to achieve the necessary concentrations, so it's easy to overfeed. Feeding levels are part of that "flick-of-the-wrist" stuff I mentioned earlier. It will take a little practice to provide just enough food without overfeeding your larvae. It's really better to judge actual food levels in the aquarium instead of just adding a certain dosage of Brine shrimp. So a "dime-sized drop of concentrated Brine shrimp" is really more of a guideline than an actual measurement. Adding too many Brine shrimp at one time is a waste of Brine shrimp, because the Peppermint shrimp larvae won't be able to eat them all before they use up their yolk reserves and molt. Then you'll just end up with loads of Brine shrimp that are a bit too big and active for your starving Peppermint shrimp to catch and eat. And if you add WAY too many Brine shrimp, your Peppermint shrimp larvae will scream and run. Too many food organisms seems to curb their appetites. **It's better to underfeed than to overfeed your larvae.**

I judge food levels in the larvae tank with a low power magnifying glass. Once the larvae and their food are well distributed around the tank, I look through the magnifying glass at one larva. There should be approximately 5 to 10 Brine shrimp nauplii within easy reach of each larva (about an inch around the larva), at least during the first week of their lives. After the second week, Peppermint shrimp transform from being passive hunters, where they have to bump into their prey, into active hunters, where they start reaching out for it. By the third week, they will actually *swim* after it! Ooo. It's like watching larval humans stand up and learn to walk. Makes me so proud! But anyway, it means that the Brine shrimp don't have to be quite as dense in the tank as the Peppermint shrimp get older (but the Brine shrimp will also be getting bigger, as you'll see in a minute).

Every day during the first week, you want to add enough newly-hatched Brine shrimp so that your Peppermint shrimp won't go hungry, but not so many that there are some leftover until the next day (more practice-makes-perfect stuff). As the hours go by, the Brine shrimp gradually use up their yolk and their value as a food item goes down. Newly-hatched Brine shrimp are bright orange because of that yolk. As they use it up their color fades to a kind of transparent gray-brown. By the next day, the Brine shrimp molt to their next stage and almost double in size and speed, making them useless as food for less-than-a-week-old Peppermint shrimp. By the end of the week, Peppermint shrimp get better at hunting and can catch and eat the slightly larger, speedier versions of Brine shrimp, but unless those Brine shrimp were fed something nutritious, you're not going to be supplying your Peppermint shrimp with enough energy to make it to their next stage in life. So the next thing you need to know is how to grow nutritious Brine shrimp to a slightly larger size.

Growing Juvenile Brine Shrimp (1 mm to 3 mm in Size)

What I do is hatch enough Brine shrimp for one or two larvae tanks, plus leftovers. I use most of the newly-hatched Brine shrimp for that day's feeding and then set up another bottle for hatching the next day's food. I dump the leftover Brine shrimp into a larger container, like a 20 gallon tank of their own, or a clean garbage can (really clean, as in new). All you need is an air stone to circulate the water well because Brine shrimp need high oxygen levels to live in high concentrations. Then you need to feed them something.

There are liquid foods at aquarium stores that advertise themselves as great foods for raising Brine shrimp. Well, yeah. Brine shrimp can live on most anything that is the right size for them to eat.

You can feed them just plain old yeast and have them survive (In fact, quite a lot of those store-bought liquid foods are yeast-based). But those foods may not make them nutritious enough for your Peppermint shrimp larvae. They'll be missing important (for Peppermint shrimp, not Brine shrimp) carotenoid proteins and fatty acids and who knows what else.

I make up my own recipe that seems to work pretty well. All I know is that starving Brine shrimp don't grow very much, and yeast-fed Brine shrimp grow better, but Peppermint shrimp larvae don't fare well on those pale yeast-fed Brine shrimp. My recipe is modified after one used by some freshwater fish breeders who use a similar recipe to raise *Daphnia* (a freshwater plankton-critter) to feed their young fish.

I mix one teaspoon of baby food pureed sweet potatoes, and one teaspoon of baby food peas into one cup of water. I usually add a drop of liquid vitamin supplement, and often for good measure, I'll add a small amount of some fatty acid enrichment mixture such as Super Selco. Then I put it all in a small resealable bottle like the kind used for soda or water and shake well.

It keeps well in the refrigerator for about a week. You should shake it each time before using it to resuspend the food particles. One cup of the mixture is enough to feed a 20 gallon container with a dense population of Brine shrimp for three days, which translates to about a shot glass of the mixture per day. If you have only a few Brine shrimp to feed, use less of the mixture. The easiest way to see just how much food your container of Brine shrimp can handle is to add just enough of the mixture to make the water *slightly* cloudy. As the young Brine shrimp feed on it, the water will clear.

So, in the beginning, when your Brine shrimp population is low, you may feed your culture container a small amount once per day. Later, as you add more leftover newly-hatched Brine shrimp to the container, and as the ones already in there grow bigger, you may find that the water clears a lot sooner. Eventually you will end up feeding about a shot glass (also known as an ounce) of mixture per day. You might even have to schedule two feedings per day if you have a lot of older Brine shrimp in there. I don't recommend feeding them more often than that or you might pollute the container too quickly. This recipe turns the young

Brine shrimp an orange-brown color and the Peppermint shrimp larvae seem to fare pretty well on them, so I assume they're nutritionally adequate.

I've also tried Martin Moe's Brand Name vegetable juice recipe and that works well too. You can find that recipe in his book, *Breeding The Orchid Dottyback*. He originally developed it as an easier way to feed rotifers, instead of constantly struggling to keep an active microalgae culture going to feed the ravenous little monsters. You can also use it to raise Brine shrimp, and Peppermint shrimp larvae survive while eating those reddish-brown Brine shrimp.

I haven't studied which of the two recipes is better nutritionally. It would seem that Moe's recipe might be, since it has more ingredients (back to that "winging it" method of providing as varied a diet as possible in hopes of hitting on the right combination). The only reason I don't consistently use that recipe is because my mother always drank the Brand Name veggie juice just when I needed it. I never had a problem with her eating the squished-veggie baby food, I don't know why.

You'll need a fine mesh net to collect the week-old Brine shrimp from their culture container. Rinse them under freshwater just like you did for the newly-hatched versions because you don't want any of their culture water in your larvae tank as a health precaution. There's always the possibility that Brine shrimp are not affected by some bacteria or fungus that grows in their culture water, but Peppermint shrimp larvae might be susceptible to it. Rinsing isn't a foolproof method of getting rid of those possible hitchhikers, but it doesn't hurt.

Since you will be constantly adding newly-hatched Brine shrimp on a daily basis, you will eventually get a large variability in the sizes of the Brine shrimp in your culture container. There will be Brine shrimp that measure anywhere from one millimeter to three or even five millimeters long if you are giving them a good growing environment. You can sort them according to size by using different mesh nets or sieves if you want, but I don't bother with that. By the time you get the largest ones, your Peppermint shrimp larvae should be old enough to be able to wrestle with them.

I have two 20 gallon food-grade buckets in the shower stall of that converted bathroom, uh, sorry, the Larval Food Culture Room. One bucket is for feeding and growing the newly-hatched Brine shrimp to what I will call the "juvenile" size (around 1 to 3 mm). The other bucket is used for "Cleaning Day". Eventually the water in the first bucket will get disgusting. An ooky slime will develop along the sides, debris will collect on the bottom, and a snotty kind of foam will coat the surface of the water. Before it gets too bad and kills off the Brine shrimp, I fill the other 20 gallon bucket with new, clean saltwater and transfer the Brine shrimp, via that fine mesh net, into their new home.

The transfer takes about twenty minutes, fifteen of which is just sitting around and waiting for the debris to settle to the bottom after turning off the air to the dirty bucket. The healthiest Brine shrimp will be doing loop-de-loops near the surface of the yellow water and it only takes about five minutes or so to scoop them all up with the fine mesh net and move them to the clean bucket. You may have to pause periodically during collection, to allow disturbed sediment to resettle.

After moving as many Brine shrimp as you can catch without catching sediment at the bottom, wash out the disgusting bucket and get it ready for the next Cleaning Day. Luckily, unless you are seriously overfeeding the culture container, Cleaning Day doesn't arrive more often than once per week. During the transfer from one bucket to the next, I usually pick out the largest Brine shrimp and move them outside to a 30 gallon garbage can. There, in an area of dappled sunlight, they can grow into adult Brine shrimp (more on that in a minute).

Since the original writing of this book, many new commercial products have appeared on the market. They are designed mainly for feeding filter feeding corals and sponges, but they also appear to work for raising Brine shrimp. Bottles of preserved microalgae work fairly well and the resulting Brine shrimp seem nutritious for the Peppermint shrimp larvae they feed.

Other commercial products (those that are not made up of preserved microalgae) have ingredients that vary from cheap pea flour to freeze dried, or otherwise preserved, oceanic plankton. Brine shrimp will grow when fed these other products, but I do not know if those

Brine shrimp will be nutritionally adequate for Peppermint shrimp larvae. I have not tested many brands yet.

Any of these commercial products are handy and easy to store, but I would still recommend adding a fatty acid enrichment and/or vitamin supplement to them as well.

Feeding Peppermint Shrimp Larvae (Part B)

I continue to mix newly-hatched Brine shrimp with juvenile Brine shrimp in the larvae tank so that all the Peppermint shrimp will be able to catch food, no matter how fast or slow they are. You should always overlap the size of the food items since not all Peppermint shrimp have the same hunting prowess. Later, starting in week 3, you should begin to mix in some adult or sub-adult (5 mm or larger) Brine shrimp because some of the larger Peppermint shrimp larvae are willing to wrestle with bulkier, feistier prey. A full-grown adult Brine shrimp is approximately 1 cm, and really only four- to five-week old Peppermint shrimp larvae can catch and hold those. Three week old Peppermint shrimp can handle juvenile/sub-adult Brine shrimp that are around 5 mm (half a centimeter) long.

The sooner you can get Peppermint shrimp larvae onto a steady diet of adult Brine shrimp, the sooner they will metamorphose into postlarvae. You can feed Peppermint shrimp newly-hatched Brine shrimp for their entire larval life and they will eventually metamorphose, but it will extend the time that they remain larvae. I really don't know why that is. Maybe adult Brine shrimp are better, nutritionally. Adult Brine shrimp are higher in protein and lower in fat than newly-hatched Brine shrimp. Also, according to *The Plankton Culture Manual*, Brine shrimp nauplii (also known as newly-hatched Brine shrimp) lack certain amino acids, but as adults, they are rich in all essential amino acids. Or, it may simply be a matter of more meat for the amount of energy put into hunting it. One adult Brine shrimp will keep a larva busy for an hour or more while it chews on it, whereas another larva being fed only newly-hatched Brine shrimp will have to continually swim around grabbing food.

It's also more work for you to keep up with the demand. By the time they are four weeks old, they can sure put away the food, just like teenage boys! If they are on a strict diet of newly-hatched Brine shrimp, you'll have to feed them two and three, maybe even four times a day! With adult Brine shrimp you can get away with just one or two times a day. By the time your Peppermint shrimp larvae reach 4 weeks of age, you should have mostly adult Brine shrimp mixed with just a few week-old Brine shrimp. You only need to have one or two adult Brine shrimp within reach of each larva. Their "reach", however has increased by that time. They will swim two or three inches for food at that age.

Growing Brine Shrimp To Adult Size
(5 mm to 1 cm)

You can use most any container you like for all stages of Brine shrimp culture. 20 gallon aquariums work fine. My only complaint about them is that they are made of glass. I prefer to use plastic buckets and garbage cans because they are cheap, they can take a lot of abuse, and they are fairly easy to dump over or move around when you need to clean them. There aren't too many 20 gallon aquariums with handles on them.

I find that a 30 gallon (or larger) garbage can works well for growing Brine shrimp to adulthood because it has enough water volume to give me a longer time between water changes, and its high sides allow a good circulation pattern without too many "dead areas" where the water doesn't move much. Make sure you have an air pump that's powerful enough to pump air all the way to the bottom of the garbage can. Good circulation is essential to raising Brine shrimp.

You can keep the adult Brine shrimp growout container indoors if you like. I have kept that same garbage can in the shower stall along with the 20 gallon "juvenile" buckets. But I have found that if you move the adult container outside to an area of partial sunlight, you can keep it from getting too hot and, as an added bonus, most times you get a bloom of planktonic algae. The algae turns the water either brown or green, depending on the species, and when that happens, the Brine shrimp growout container is basically care-free. You can almost sit back with popcorn and watch them grow. I don't recommend that. It's pretty boring. The algae feeds the Brine shrimp and takes care of their poop at the same time. While the growout container is outdoors and there's an algae bloom in it, I never had to clean out the container.

Eventually though, as the Brine shrimp grow, so do their appetites, and you may have to supplement their diet of algae with some of your homemade Brine shrimp food (or preserved microalgae, or whatever other product). Observe the water color. If the water starts to clear up, then your Brine shrimp are probably eating their food supply too quickly. When you start adding the homemade Brine shrimp food, you'll have to watch for that snotty foam to let you know when the water needs changing. An indoor container develops that foam within one to two weeks. Outdoors, it takes a bit longer. If you add a sponge filter to the garbage can, you can go even longer before you have to clean it out.

With this method, you will have a choice of Brine shrimp sizes to feed the Peppermint shrimp larvae as they grow. You should give them various-sized Brine shrimp all the way to metamorphosis.

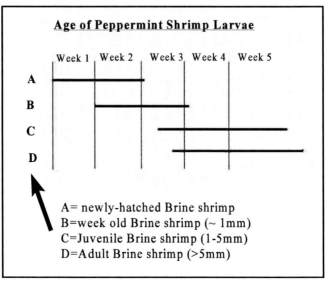

**Brine shrimp ages & sizes should overlap as
Peppermint shrimp grow.**

ALTERNATIVE FOODS

Some people don't like to use living food items because the culture work is a hassle. Peppermint shrimp larvae will eat other things such as shaved frozen food or commercial shrimp larvae chow. It seems a lot easier to just open up a canister or the freezer and sprinkle food into the tank.

Live foods are preferable to inert foods because they stay in the water column, keeping themselves on the menu, whereas dead or prepared foods eventually drift down to the bottom, out of reach. After inert foods fall to the bottom, they quickly decompose and degrade the water quality. When you use something other than living prey items, you will have to do a lot more "housekeeping chores" and you have to give your larvae a lot more personal attention in the form of feeding them all the time. So you have to make a choice about which method is more work for you.

The main reason I am offering this section on alternative foods is because lately there has been some problems with Brine shrimp eggs. That convenient hatch-on-demand food source is getting less convenient.

It seems we humans (surprise, surprise) are screwing around with the environment around those salty lakes where the Brine shrimp live. Developments around those lakes has increased runoff into the waters. That runoff adds things like pesticides to the water. But even when it's something that seems fairly innocuous, like simple rainwater (or melting snow), it can have an effect. During 1997, 1998 and 1999, the harvest of Brine shrimp cysts was very low to none. The ones they did collect were poor quality. The blame was placed on El Niño, which caused excessive snow that melted and ran into the lakes and decreased the salinity. Brine shrimp produce live young when the salinity levels are lower, which translates into very few to no Brine shrimp cysts drifting to shore to be collected and canned.

Since virtually all of the aquaculture industry uses Brine shrimp in some part of their culture work, there's a bit of a panic going on. The price of Brine shrimp eggs has skyrocketed. The good quality eggs — the ones that have a dependable hatch rate — are shipped to the aquaculture industry while the poorer quality eggs are given to the aquarium industry. So those cans with the suddenly high prices that you see in the aquarium stores are packed with older eggs, or eggs of lesser quality, that don't give a reliable hatching. A lot of those eggs fail to hatch, and when you do get some to hatch, it's difficult to separate the few Brine shrimp nauplii from the thousands of unhatched eggs that clot up near the bottom of the hatching container.

With hundreds of hungry larvae to feed, it was frustrating to go to the cupboard (or Larval Food Culture Room) and find that it was bare. I lost a lot of larvae due to starvation when I didn't get the amount of Brine shrimp that I expected to hatch. I began to depend more and more on prepared foods.

There are commercial feeds for shrimp larvae. They are designed for the kind of shrimp that you eat. There are three problems with those kinds of foods. First, they grow the Eatin'-type shrimp on farms with humongous ponds, where they deal with shrimp populations that number in the millions. That means that they package those larval foods in amounts that are *way* too much for the average aquarist. Second is that Eatin' shrimp larvae hatch out in a more primitive stage than Peppermint shrimp larvae. They feed on much smaller foods throughout most of their larval life. And third, well, Morris the cat ain't as finicky as larval Peppermint shrimp. After finally getting a hold of some commercial larvae food — several different brands, in fact — I'd watch (even yelling at the stupid little things, as if that helps) as they'd grab a morsel of food, give it a test-chew, drop it, and decide that starvation was a better choice. What do they put in those foods? Brussels sprouts? If my mom had forced me to eat brussels sprouts as a kid, I guess I might have chosen starvation as the way out, too.

The solution to the first problem comes from some aquaculture supply houses that are willing to subdivide their feeds into one pound containers and charge you a ridiculous amount of money for the privilege. One pound of larval food will go a *looong* way.

Problem two, food size, is easy to overcome. You ignore the recommendations and give your larval Peppermint shrimp the postlarval feeds. It's a larger size that your Peppermint shrimp will prefer. The smaller food particles will just be ignored by your shrimp and will only contribute to the pollution levels in your tank.

The third problem, finicky eaters, well, that just takes time and patience to find out which brand they like. For the record, I did finally find one brand that they would sort of eat. I received it as a sample and couldn't get it in small quantities, and it spoiled very quickly, so I said (well, never mind what I said) and gave up on all commercial larval shrimp feeds.

So, back to what works. The frozen food mixture that I feed to adult Peppermint shrimp works, but it pollutes the tank way too much to be seriously considered. If you want to try it, take a knife and shave off some of the frozen food into the water. Peppermint shrimp larvae young and old like frozen food bits, and 4-week-olds will swim a long way to grab a piece of it (a long distance to a 4 week old larval shrimp is approximately 3 inches). A welcome change to the commercial feed fiasco(s). The biggest problem with frozen food, other than the oils and proteins that instantly accumulate on the water surface, is that it drops almost immediately towards the bottom of the tank. Once it is at the bottom, it's useless. And you'll have to change the water and clean the bottom quite frequently in order to keep the shrimp larvae from "dropping like flies" a couple of hours after dinner.

So here's the best solution to the alternative larval food problem. Are you ready? It's really mind-blowing. It's cheap, it's easy to find, it's nutritious and handy and it doesn't spoil very quickly. It's (drum roll please)... *Flake food.*

Yes, that's right. That same time-tested stuff that's sitting on the shelves in virtually every pet store around. Yes, there's a big variety and yes, the Peppermint shrimp are still picky about which brands they'll eat. But damn, it's a lot cheaper and easier to find out which those are.

I recommend reading labels first. Like any good parent, you should be concerned about what your kids eat. Again, I like the variety approach. The more ingredients the flake food has, the better (I hope) that it is. I like the kinds that have more "meat" to them, especially if it's listed near the beginning of the ingredients list. The foods that promote color seem to have the best ingredients so far. The cheapest color food on the market has fish meal as its first ingredient, followed very closely by shrimp meal, fish oil, lecithin (a very important ingredient for crustaceans), krill meal, crab meal, crayfish meal, and spirulina algae, among other ingredients.

After you've picked a likely food, you can try it out on your larvae. If you are working only with flake food and not a combination of Brine shrimp and flake food, you'll need to feed your shrimp larvae more often. During the first two days of larval life you will need to powder the flake food by rolling it between your fingers. What that does is provide a multitude of sizes for the shrimp larvae to pick from, since not all the flakes between your fingers will get crushed to powder. Some of the larvae will prefer to eat the larger flakes, holding on to them even as they sink to the bottom. Others will prefer slightly smaller morsels of food that they can manipulate.

You should seriously observe the larvae right after you feed them. Get a magnifying glass so you can monitor how they take to your brand of flake food. If they like it, you'll see most of the larvae hugging food particles. You should see them actively chewing on the particles. If they don't like your food, they'll nibble on it and soon drop it.

During the first two or three days after hatching, you will have to overfeed the tank in order to get enough food drifting downward through the water for the larvae to bump into. Remember that they are passive hunters, if you can call them hunters, at that stage. You have to provide enough food at each feeding to make sure that all the larvae bump into something to eat, and then you have to repeat that several times throughout the day so that they get enough food each day. They should get a minimum of three feedings, but they really should get five or more feedings per day if you are relying solely on non-living food.

After several feedings of a likely brand of flake food (one that you believe they are eating), use that magnifying glass to see if there are any fecal strands (shrimp doodies) coming out of the southern end of northbound larvae. If your magnifying glass is strong enough, you might be able to look through the transparent bodies of the larvae themselves and see the line of fecal material making its way toward the tail. If you see shrimp poop, it's a good indication that they aren't fooling you. They really are eating that brand of food, not just playing with it.

It's only during the first week that you have to overfeed them. The food particles, in the meantime, will accumulate in great heaps on the bottom of the tank. I realize that I already said that you don't have to do any bottom cleaning during the first week, only water additions, but I lied. That applies only if you are using live food or a combination of living and non-living foods.

If the food particles haven't covered the bottom, you might be able to get away with just adding water instead of siphoning the bottom clean, but if the gunk gets too thick, you'll notice (if you're really looking. They *are* pretty hard to see that first week) the larvae starting to become trapped in it. That's when you have to vacuum the bottom clean. Good luck. If you don't vacuum the bottom, you may simply notice that there doesn't seem to be any larvae left in the tank and there are plenty of white corpses lolling about on the bottom. You no longer need to feed them at that point.

I actually prefer to use a combination of newly-hatched Brine shrimp and powdered flake food during the first week. Live prey stays in the water column so the larvae have something to snack on between meals, and the bottom doesn't get so cluttered so fast. With poor quality Brine shrimp eggs that give a low hatch rate, you will have a hard time providing enough Brine shrimp to give your Peppermint shrimp larvae a full day's supply of nutrition, but you *can* get enough Brine shrimp nauplii to provide the day-long, between-meals snacks.

After the first week, you can offer them larger flakes. They are really attracted to large objects, especially ones that smell good, so don't be afraid to offer a flake that's three times the size of a larva. Two, three, and four larvae will share one flake. If you can provide the live Brine shrimp for the between-meals snacks, you should. Then you can get away with only two flake food meals per day. If you simply sprinkle the flakes on the water surface, they will gradually get wet and sink one by one so that there is a near constant stream of flakes drifting down towards the bottom. That stretches out the mealtime.

It also — here's a hint — teaches your larvae that food comes from the surface. This is a book on how to raise *and train* your Peppermint shrimp. I'll bet you never thought it would include shrimp larvae. By the second or third week, the larvae (or at least 80% of them, since some of them remain pretty dumb) will begin to turn upside-down (or is that right-side-up, since they normally swim head down?) and fumble around on the surface of the water when they smell food. This behavior is handy because it not only allows you to drop food right into each larva's grasp, but the training follows them right on through metamorphosis, and you'll have newly-settled Peppermint shrimp that will come to the surface and eat out of your hand. Well, let me modify that a little. Newly-settled Peppermint shrimp act a little confused and scared for the first few days until they get used to their new bodies, and *then* they will swim up to the water surface to eat out of your hand.

I have brought larvae through metamorphosis on flake food alone, but it's a lot of work. The constant feeding and cleaning takes a bunch of fun out of the hobby. A combination of live Brine shrimp and flake food makes things a bit easier.

Once your Peppermint shrimp settle to the bottom, you can treat them like tiny (very tiny) adults. They eat the same foods and behave in the same ways as the adult shrimp.

There's one more note to make before I move on to the next chapter: the flake foods that promote color do seem to do what they advertise. Larvae fed only Brine shrimp develop a pinkish hue that you really only notice as they get larger. Larvae fed color-promoting flake food, or a combination of flake food and Brine shrimp develop a pinkish color very early on and turn almost red by the fourth week of their lives. I haven't noticed much of a difference in color after they settle, but by then they are being fed the same frozen concoction.

Summary

What a deal. This book comes complete with its own version of Cliff's notes. Here's the short version of the previous chapters.

Set up a 20 gallon "spawning tank" with a basic filtration system such as an undergravel filter and an outside power filter. Stock the tank with 2-6 adult Peppermint shrimp.

Set the timer so that the aquarium lights are on at least 12 hours each day. Keep the room temperature stable, or use an aquarium heater to avoid fluctuations in water temperature. The preferred water temperature is 78-82 F.

Feed the adult shrimp at least twice, or better yet, three times daily with high quality foods.

Construct a Larvae Collector, or learn how to function under extreme sleep deprivation.

Prepare the Larvae Tank. You'll need a clean, bare 20 gallon aquarium with an airstone in one corner and a light on a timer. Leave the aquarium empty until it is needed. Cover the sides with a dark material to keep out stray light and to provide contrast to make the larvae and their foods easier to observe. Folks in cooler climates may need to have an aquarium heater handy.

Hatching day: Move the larvae to a separate container. Fill the Larvae Tank with 4 to 6 inches of water from the Spawning Tank. Gently pour the larvae into their new home. Adjust the air flow to give a gentle circulation. If using a submersible aquarium heater, keep it under the water, but raise it up off the bottom a bit to prevent larvae from becoming trapped underneath it. Feed the larvae.

Trickle in one gallon per day until the Larvae Tank is completely filled. You may need to adjust the air flow as the water level changes. Add new food daily. Monitor food levels carefully. As the tank fills, suspend the heater away from the bottom and sides of the aquarium, if possible, to prevent larvae from becoming trapped.

After the Larvae Tank has been filled, begin the daily (or weekly) bottom cleaning regime. Replace the water lost during the vacuuming procedures with new, clean saltwater.

Add live food, if you are using live food, after cleaning the tank to replenish populations lost during the vacuuming procedures.

Repeat the previous two steps for 3 to 5 more weeks.

Cheer for any larvae that survive your care and metamorphose at last into little postlarvae. Throw a metamorphosis party for them. Ignore other people's quizzical stares. After 5 to 8 weeks of effort, feel free to celebrate.

Convince those same people that you are truly nuts when you tell them you're going to try to train your shrimp. Ignore their next question: *"Why?"*

Troubleshooting

Although there is no *way* I can cover all the problems you could encounter while raising shrimp larvae, I am going to try to mention the most common problems or questions you may have and suggest some possible solutions. I am only going to consider problems with larval rearing as that's where most of your difficulties and frustrations may arise. Other problems concerning the adult shrimp fall within basic aquarium care and maintenance which many other books deal with in detail.

One important concept that the troubleshooting sections of many other books neglect: what *normal* is. You should recognize what healthy behaviors look like, so that you'll know when you are seeing unhealthy behaviors. As mentioned elsewhere in this book, healthy shrimp larvae swim with their tails oriented towards the light source. Usually that means they swim with their heads down and their tails pointed toward the water surface. They paddle their future "walking" legs to maneuver around.

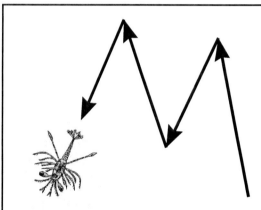

Healthy Behaviors:
Once the larvae develop their "spear-legs", they begin a more active hunting style. They swim upwards a short distance, then "pounce" downwards. They will repeat this until they capture a food item.

Once they have grown their spear-legs, you will see new behaviors developing. They begin to swim in a steady up and down pattern. They will swim upward a short distance, then "pounce" downward. This is the beginning of their more active hunting style. They no longer passively run into their food; they begin to reach out for it on that downstroke. As they get older, they develop better aim.

Watching the angle of the spear-legs can alert you to unhealthy behaviors, which can help you to head off disaster. Healthy larvae hold their spear-legs generally pointed toward their tails, or at least some angle between the horizontal position and their tails. Unhealthy or stressed larvae generally hold their spear-legs pointed more toward their heads (or some angle between the horizontal position and their heads). The stressed larvae may still eat and swim just fine, but the angle of their spear-legs is an early warning sign that you have some kind of water quality or disease issue developing.

Let me make one addendum to the spear-leg observations. 4-6 week old

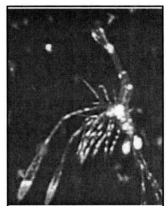

Observing the angle of the spear-legs will help to anticipate potential problems.
Downward-pointing spear legs is an early sign of general stress.

larvae have greatly elongated spear-legs, and tend to hold them with a kind of "kink" in the middle, so that the paddle-like portion functions like a stabilizing rudder. While the "rudder" itself might point towards the head of the larva, the angle of the first part of the spear-leg still points in the direction of the tail on healthy larvae. So it's the angle of the spear-leg *from the body attachment site* that matters most. When stressed 4-6 week old larvae drop that first part of the spear-leg downwards, just as in the photo above, then the large stabilizing rudder will begin to malfunction, which initiates a rotating or spinning swimming behavior. Pretty good sign that something's not right.

While reading the following troubleshooting chart, you may notice that my first recommendation for any problem is to make a water change — sometimes a large one, sometimes a small one, but always a water change. There are a few reasons for that.

Stress of any kind suppresses an organism's immune system. If you are fairly healthy, you may be able to fight off that cold virus that's circulating around your office at work, but if you haven't slept well lately, and/or you have been speed-feeding a lot of junk food instead of real nutrition in order to meet some deadline... well, all that compromises your immune system and makes you a little more vulnerable to infection. Stress comes in many forms. There's physical stress, such as starvation or a poor diet or exhaustion. For humans there's mental stress, but I don't think I want to get into the psychology of a shrimp larva. And there's environmental stress, which for aquatic critters means having to put up with poor water quality. Whenever you encounter *any* problem with your larvae, your first response should be to change some of the water in the tank. The best form of preventative medicine and basic treatment for disease and stress is a good environment.

When your larvae are under attack by disease-causing organisms, they shouldn't also be battling poor water quality. So the first thing a water change does is reduce any stress due to some unidentified water quality problem. Pollution is pretty obvious if the water's cloudy and there's plenty of debris on the bottom. But even if the water looks clean and clear to you, there may be something even more subtle that affects aquatic critters. Sometimes mild stress can be caused by the depletion or imbalance of certain trace elements in the aquarium water. All organisms require various trace elements in differing quantities. The algae and bacteria coating the sides of the aquarium, the Brine shrimp, and the Peppermint shrimp larvae are all competing for tiny amounts of chemicals such as iodine or zinc, or even arsenic. After a while the water chemistry in the tank can get a little out of balance, lacking certain elements while having too much of others. If you just randomly add trace element supplements, you could be replacing some of the missing elements, but you could also be adding more of some chemical that's already in abundance. Removing some of the old tank water and replacing it with newly-made saltwater, which has the right ratios of elements and duplicates ocean water, re-balances the water chemistry in your aquarium.

Another possible benefit from a water change is to decrease the population of the disease organism (or toxin) that's circulating about in the aquarium. It might give the larvae time to regain some strength to deal with the problem, sort of like boxers taking time-outs to sit down and recover a little between rounds.

Sometimes a water change is not enough. When problem-causing microorganisms are just overrunning the aquarium, whether the larvae are being attacked directly or whether something lining the tank walls is producing some toxin, then you have to get the larvae out of that situation. If you move the larvae to a new tank of good clean water, they might have a chance of recovering. Also, if you believe that microorganisms are the cause of the problem, then sterilize everything that goes into the new tank. That means air hoses, air stones, nets, hands, whatever.

I have found that most times just improving the water quality and lowering the population density of disease organisms can help the larvae to overcome the problem on their own, without drugs. I only avoid the use of antibiotics and other chemicals because I have found that crustacean larvae are so sensitive to certain antibiotics that it is both easier and more effective to just move the larvae one by one to a new, sterile aquarium. Also, if you don't have the facilities or equipment available for proper identification of the disease organisms, then your diagnoses and treatment will be random guesswork.

I actually prefer to stop problems before they start *(hey, there's a concept)*, kind of like preventative medicine. In Asia, many shrimp farms practice something called probiotics. Maybe you've heard of it, maybe you haven't. I first learned of the concept while watching *The Wizard of Oz* as a kid, I just didn't know it back then. I learned, along with Dorothy, that not all witches are bad. There are good witches and there are bad witches. Likewise, there are good bacteria and there are bad bacteria.

The glass walls of your aquarium are home to all sorts of bacteria (imagine thousands of itty-bitty apartments along the tank walls). What you would like to have is for the sides of the aquarium to be colonized by harmless microorganisms, which will keep the bad ones from moving in and ruining the neighborhood. You can specifically add beneficial bacteria (now found in bottles at your local aquarium store) to your tank in the first few days after you begin filling it, in hopes of giving that "good guy" population a head start over the bad ones.

PROBLEM	POSSIBLE CAUSE	SOLUTION
The water is a cloudy, whitish color, and it's staying that way.	White cloudy water is a sign of a bacterial bloom.	Make a larger than normal water change. If the problem persists or worsens, or if the larvae are struggling, move the larvae to a new, clean tank. Or, remove the larvae to a separate container, sterilize their tank & fill with new saltwater, replace the larvae.
The water is a murky green or brown color.	Colors other than white indicate a bloom of planktonic algae.	Most times, algae blooms are not harmful unless they become too dense. If it is difficult to see the back of the tank, make a larger than normal water change.
One or two larvae are swimming with difficulty. Seem to have a hard time determining which way is up.	Possible loss of equilibrium due to damaged "spear-leg(s)".	Not much to do about this one except hope they live through to their next molt, which will repair the damage. Check the air flow & bubble size to make sure that it's not damaging the larvae.

PROBLEM	POSSIBLE CAUSE	SOLUTION
Larvae dying or disappearing. All seem healthy but each day there are fewer.	Check sides of tank carefully for stinging hydroid colonies &/or medusae (tiny jellyfish). Often introduced via natural seawater or from tanks with "live rock".	Hydroids form small whitish colonies along the tank walls & medusae may be their offspring. There's not much you can do for an infestation since any chemical treatments affect the shrimp larvae as well. Hydroids can be scraped off & siphoned out, but it always seems you miss some. Better just to move the larvae one by one to a new tank.
All (or most) of the larvae are spinning and/or seem hyperactive.	Unknown cause. Possible toxin in the water.	Moving the larvae to a different tank with new, clean saltwater usually clears up this problem. If you don't move them, they can live for weeks while spinning, but it inhibits their hunting ability. Usually die before metamorphosis.
Larva(e) having molting problems. Not completely escaping old exoskeleton and/or missing limbs or eyes.	Possible iodine or calcium deficiency.	You can add supplements, or you can make (do I sound like a broken record yet?) a small water change.

PROBLEM	POSSIBLE CAUSE	SOLUTION
One larva (or more) is folded in half and/or doing calisthenics.	Larva just molted.	Do nothing. It's perfectly normal. Usually only happens during "serious" molts, where some drastic new change has occurred, such as getting stalked eyes. I wonder if it's painful.
Larvae appear weak. Having trouble swimming. Appendages are coated with white stuff.	Possible bacteria or fungus-amongus.	If it's a surface coating of bacteria, it will correct itself with a thorough tank cleaning and a molt. If it's a fungus, gee, that's too bad. They're probably not gonna make it. Be sure to sterilize everything after they're gone. Commercial shrimp farms often add *Treflan* to reduce incidence of fungal infections.
Larvae have lost all color. Larvae are white.	Unknown cause. Could be a vicious microbe (bacteria, virus, fungus).	Larvae usually die within 24 hours. Changing the water or moving larvae to a new tank doesn't help. Sterilize everything after they die.
Hair algae on tank sides is tangling & trapping larvae	High amounts of nutrients in water.	Thoroughly clean the tank bottom & sides, removing as much algae as possible. Make a large water change. Re-evaluate your feeding & cleaning practices.

Training Your Shrimp

> **WARNING:** This section may convince your family that you need professional help.

The shrimp brain consists of three fused neurons, so we're not talking about high IQ's here. The "training" of your shrimp will be at best modified natural behaviors, such as food gathering and parasite-picking. So please don't expect to start your own Marine World and have exciting shrimp shows. (Wow, if only you could train a shrimp to tail-walk like dolphins across the surface of the water! Hmmm... Well, maybe that'll be in the *next* edition...)

As mentioned earlier, the shrimp should have an aquarium all to themselves, because active fish make them nervous. Shrimp aren't real smart, but they're not that stupid, either. Any shrimp that stays out in the open and acts strangely is begging to be eaten. Wild-caught shrimp are only slightly more difficult to train than homegrown ones, but they can still be trained. They just have to have more time to realize that they are alone in a tank devoid of predators, and that you are the food delivery service. Once they get a little braver, then you can start working with them.

Homegrown shrimp, on the other hand, have never experienced predators, and although they still have their instincts that tell them to flee from quick movements, they don't jump as far away and are willing to come back and investigate almost immediately. All of your movements should be slow ones. No matter how much you've worked with the shrimp, they still spook fairly easily.

I'm going to describe these "training" techniques as if you are working with wild-caught shrimp, since they take more time and patience. Homegrown Peppermint shrimp are a lot easier to try new things out on.

The first "trick" will be to get the shrimp to eat from your hand. This is the simplest one. First, go wash your hands, especially if you just got through working on the car and you have black grease all the way up to your elbow. You should already know not to stick sweaty, icky hands into an aquarium, but just in case you don't, now you do. You're going to spend a long time with your hand under the water, so it shouldn't be dirty. Working with wild-caught shrimp will tax your patience. Homegrown shrimp may eat from your hand almost immediately. Training the shrimp to eat from your hand is not only mildly entertaining, but it is quite helpful when checking out the status of their eggs.

You need to take something particularly yummy, like a portion of that frozen mixture, and pinch it between your fingers. Hold it near the bottom, close to the shrimp and then don't move. Once they get brave and start picking at the food, slowly move your hand away from the bottom of the aquarium so that the shrimp have to leave the comfort of their rocks and swim up for the food. Gradually, over a few days, the shrimp will come to expect food from your hand and will come out of their homes upon seeing you. It still may take some time to get them to come to the surface for food, though. If you trained your larvae to search the surface of the water for food, then your homegrown Peppermint shrimp may already be there, paddling around upside-down, almost walking on the surface of the water. You don't really have to "teach" them. Eventually, even wild-caught Peppermint shrimp will begin to dance excitedly under the water surface when they see you arrive. Amaze your friends and neighbors!

Actually, since I said that, I have to mention that you need to teach your shrimp to do this in front of other people, too. Did you ever see that cartoon of the man who found a singing, dancing, frog? Every time he tried to show his amazing frog to other people, it just sat there and belched. Yes, that will happen with your shrimp, too. Well, maybe not the belching part, but they might sit back in their caves and wonder who that stranger next to you is.

The shrimp do seem to recognize individuals — which doesn't seem right given their brain capacity — but my shrimp run toward the front of the tank, impatient for food when I show up, but they ignore my husband when he looks in the tank. And in our home aquarium, where he is the primary feeder, they ignore me and run out when he shows up. So you should get them used to having other people and/or other movements going on outside the tank while you're feeding them, so that you can share the fun occasionally. Maybe try to have other people hand-feed your shrimp. If you get people to join you for this kind of entertainment they have a harder time making fun of you behind your back.

Once the shrimp really trust you, you can move on to the next step, which is to cup your hand and gently lift the shrimp out of the water with only the tiniest amount of water to make them comfortable. I don't keep them out of the water for long since gravity squashes them flat and helpless. But they will tolerate it for a short while if they trust you not to leave them there. Betray their trust even one time, scare them too much by keeping them out for too long, and they'll never let you do it again. Imagine if someone held you underwater until you thought you might drown. How much would you trust them to do it again?

Once you have them used to quick journeys out of the water, they don't mind so much when various body parts like their antennae, eyes and rostrums stick out of the water while you feed them. With time, you can put some food in your cupped hand, so that it floats in a little puddle of water separated from the aquarium water. Once the shrimp realize there's food there, at least one will learn to make the short trip over the outside edge of your hand, which is out of the water, and land in the middle of your hand where the food is in just a puddle of water. Usually it's only one brave shrimp that will do this trick. Its reward is a bunch of food that it can eat without any of the others trying to steal it. There, with only the lower portion of its body submerged it will greedily stuff its face while other body parts like eyes and antennae stick out of the water.

These aren't truly amazing tricks to the average human being. Ordinary folks might watch and say, whoopty-do — and then start hiding all the sharp objects in the house. But to anyone who knows anything about normal shrimp behavior, that's pretty cool. Okay, maybe I need to get out more.

Yes, you can get the shrimp to swim through a hoop, but it's really more accident than design. Normally, when training other kinds of animals, you reward them very quickly after they perform some action and after a while they get the idea that the two things are connected. Action = reward. Shrimp don't ever seem to "get it". There's a hoop, they crawl or paddle through it, and you feed them, but they don't seem to understand the cause and effect part of that experiment. To their minds, the hoop is really just some sort of object to play on (and through) while waiting to be fed. C'mon, they do only have three fused neurons. Give 'em a break!

Notes on Other Species

Along with Peppermint shrimp, I raised, or rather, attempted to raise, two other species of shrimp as part of an effort to get rich the hard way. One was *Lysmata amboinensis,* also called the Striped Cleaner shrimp, Scarlet Cleaner shrimp, Skunk Cleaner shrimp and many other names that try to mention that racing stripe that runs down the shrimp's back. The other was *Lysmata debelius,* also known as the Flame shrimp, the Fire shrimp, Hawaiian Red shrimp and a bunch of other names that generally call it red. Can you see why scientists use Latin names? No matter where in the world you go, no matter what the language, the Latin name of a creature never changes. *Lysmata debelius* is *Lysmata debelius* whether you're in the U.S., or Japan, or France or anywhere else. For this discussion, I'll use "Striped Cleaner shrimp" For *L. amboinensis,* and "Flame shrimp" for *L. debelius.*

I never succeeded in completing the life cycle of either of these two species during my commercial experiments. I got pretty close, though. I will discuss what I *did* accomplish and maybe that will help those of you who are attempting to raise them.

Note for the Second Edition: I have experimented, off and on, over the years since this book was first published. This chapter includes additional information, not just on *Lysmata debelius* and *L. amboinenesis,* but on a few other species as well.

Striped Cleaner Shrimp
(Lysmata amboinensis)

First, *Lysmata amboinensis,* the Striped Cleaner shrimp. Breeding them is not a problem. This species changes sex over time. They start out as males and later change into females, so if you get a large one and a small one, you will have a definite pair. Later, after the smaller shrimp catches up in size with the larger female, both shrimp may eventually produce fertile eggs but the original "female" will still be the main producer. Most times she will produce the larger batches of eggs. If you follow the procedures for breeding Peppermint shrimp, you'll have a weekly supply of larvae from one pair of Cleaner shrimp. The "male" and "female" will lay eggs on alternate weeks.

They aren't as social as the Peppermint shrimp, although in the wild, groups of Striped Cleaner shrimp can be found together in caves. That may be because in the wild they have room to escape from one another. I have found that if you keep more than one pair in a 20 gallon tank, the dominant pair will beat up and eventually eat the other two. If you have a larger tank, the two pairs can live peacefully together. I've never tried to keep a colony of Striped Cleaner shrimp. Sometimes creatures that are belligerent with each other when there is more than one pair can sort of get along when there are plenty of others around. Sure, they might pick on each other, but no single individual gets hammered. The aggression is divided up among the group.

Except for pigmentation, Cleaner shrimp larvae are physically almost identical to Peppermint shrimp. They molt approximately every two days and they have nearly identical stages. The larvae have a yellowish cast to them, and they look a little slimmer when compared to Peppermint shrimp larvae. Although anatomically they are similar, behaviorally they are not at all like Peppermint shrimp larvae. They don't seem to like to grab at larger objects like Peppermint shrimp larvae do. You can raise the Cleaner shrimp larvae on newly-hatched Brine shrimp, but you will lose significant numbers of them during the first week. Only the largest and most willing to grab Brine shrimp will survive. You will get more to survive if you raise rotifers to feed them for at least the first one or two stages. The *Plankton Culture Manual* gives loads of details on the process of rotifer-raising (and Brine shrimp culture as well). You can also get Cleaner shrimp larvae to eat powdered flake food, just like the Peppermint shrimp larvae, but they will ignore the larger flakes and only eat the tiniest particles.

They are more troublesome than Peppermint shrimp when it comes to using flake food, or any food for that matter, because they are even more passive than Peppermint shrimp. About 90% of the flake food will drop to the bottom of the tank, untouched. You have to almost continuously dribble the powdered flakes for several minutes until all the larvae have grabbed something. They have to get bumped by food two or three times before they can successfully grab it. They try, but they just have a slow reaction time.

Even when they are large enough to switch to newly-hatched Brine shrimp, you need to keep a higher concentration in the tank during that first week. Instead of 5 to 10 organisms or food particles in the inch of water surrounding a larva, you need to make sure there is a minimum of 10 food items in that same space. They also have to bump into their food for a longer period of time, so you have to keep food levels a little higher in the tank in order for them to bump into food often enough. So where Peppermint shrimp larvae begin to "reach out" for food starting on the second week, the Cleaner shrimp larvae don't start to reach for food items until much later in the second week. When they begin "reaching out" for food items, you can lower the concentrations a little.

You have to keep the bottom of the tank super-clean. Cleaner shrimp larvae tangle in debris more readily than Peppermint shrimp larvae do. They also seem more susceptible to a certain bacteria or fungus that clings to the legs of the larvae. If water conditions are not pristine, they soon have trouble swimming due to the white strands on their legs and, within a day or two, they succumb to either the infection or exhaustion.

If you can keep the larvae alive past the second week, they become hardier, and survive well until the sixth week. Then the larvae stop developing. They continue to molt and grow, but no new appliances are added. The larvae grow and grow until some measure one inch from tip of antennae to the tip of the "spear-legs" (that's *way* larger than Peppermint shrimp just before they metamorphose). Gradually the Striped shrimp larvae die off, one by one, until about week 10 when the last one croaks. That may be due to water quality problems that developed in my larvae tanks over time, since, apparently, at least two research institutions have raised these larvae through metamorphosis. They say it takes twelve to sixteen weeks to complete the larval cycle. They did *not* give any other details. Research institutions can be a little slow in divulging information if the information they discover is commercially valuable.

So, it could be that over time the water quality in my larvae tanks degraded to a point where Striped Cleaner shrimp larvae could no longer survive, *or*, it's possible that the larvae were waiting for a chemical cue to tell them it was time to settle down. Other invertebrates have the ability to postpone the final metamorphic molt — the stage where they can become postlarvae — until they receive some chemical or physical cue that tells them the habitat is perfect for them. Sometimes that chemical cue can come from certain kinds of corals or algae. For example, Abalone larvae search for a certain kind of red algae. If you take some of that algae, put it in a blender and drip the juices into a tank of competent larvae, then presto, within hours they begin to settle to the bottom. Spiny lobster larvae look for patches of an algae called *Laurencia*. Fiddler crab larvae have been shown to prefer sand that adult Fiddler crabs have sifted through, to plain sand. Barnacle larvae search for chemical cues that signal adult barnacle colonies.

Or, like in the case of *Penaeus duorarum* (now called *Farfantepenaeus duorarum*), the Florida Pink shrimp (one of the kinds you eat at restaurants), they could be waiting for a change in salinity to indicate the appropriate habitat. I have tried to find out where — exactly — Striped Cleaner shrimp live in the wild. Most books (and people) use vague, unhelpful terms like "Indo-Pacific reefs" or, "on a reef, dude". Nobody could tell me if those reefs are found near rivers, or even where on a reef these shrimp are found. On the fore reef where the waves are crashing? On the lagoon just inside the reef? That would help indicate what kinds of corals or algae are in the areas the shrimp like to inhabit.

Only one book has said that they are sometimes found in association with a *Heteractis* anemone. The Atlantic version of the Striped cleaner shrimp, *Lysmata grabhami*, is often seen around the anemone *Stoichactis helianthus*. One possible quasi-scientific method might be to grind up the anemone, drip the juices into the tank and see what happens. That seems awfully cruel and expensive and wasteful, so I'd probably prefer to keep the anemone in another tank and exchange water with the larvae tank. Or maybe keep the anemone in a mesh basket floating in the larvae tank for a time. If you're working with these shrimp, good luck, and if you should succeed in getting any of the larvae to settle, please write to me (or at least write an article for an aquarium magazine and crow about your success). I'm dying to know.

Additional information for the new edition of this book:

I have left the previous description untouched from its original edition, as it pretty much is still accurate as is. I will add a few more notes here, based on subsequent larval rearing experiments. I have still not succeeded in getting Cleaner shrimp larvae to settle, although they seem so very close. By approximately 6 weeks, they appear competent to metamorphose into postlarvae. I continue to suspect that they require some kind of chemical cue to stimulate settlement.

One fairly important observation I have made: the food you feed the adults makes a *huge* difference in larval quality and survival. Peppermint shrimp adults are fairly easily pleased, and will produce plenty of eggs and healthy, active larvae on most any food you give them. Cleaner shrimp, on the other hand, will produce eggs and larvae on most diets, but for good strong larvae, you should feed the adults a diet that is high in carotenoid proteins, such as astaxanthin. Krill, salmon, and a new dietary additive called Naturose™ have high levels of astaxanthin.

After several weeks of a high carotenoid protein diet, you may notice that newly laid eggs (and perhaps the parents themselves) take on bolder colors, and the larvae that hatch from those eggs are much more active. They will be much stronger swimmers, less prone to entanglement in bottom debris, as they will be swimming higher in the water column.

These more active larvae will make more of an attempt to eat newly-hatched Brine shrimp right away, however, they still prefer to grab at smaller food particles. At this time, I feed less-than-week-old Cleaner shrimp larvae a combination of foods. They get rotifers, plus a small dose of preserved microalgae as their "staple" initial food. I also add a small number of newly-hatched Brine shrimp for the more ambitious larvae. Several times throughout the day I also add finely ground flake foods or freeze-dried foods that are high in carotenoid proteins. Examples of such foods are freeze-dried krill or a fairly new product called Cyclopeeze™, which is freeze-dried Arctic copepods that contain lots of astaxanthin.

Other individuals working with Cleaner shrimp have observed larvae under a microscope and have seen microalgae in the larval intestines. Now, whether this was accidental ingestion or not is unknown. Also unknown is whether or not the larvae obtained nutrition from the microalgae they ingested.

In my observations under a microscope, I have not seen any appendages that make me believe they might be filter feeders. Other crustacean species that have larvae that feed on microalgae and bacteria have hairy appendages designed for sweeping tiny food particles into their mouths. Cleaner shrimp larvae do not look much different from Peppermint shrimp larvae, beyond pigmentation and a slightly more lithe build. They appear to have mainly the "grabbing-style" leg architecture, designed for holding food particles to their mouthparts. So I suspect that microalgae ingestion may be accidental. In my systems, the microalgae mainly serves to feed the rotifers and keep them nutritious until they are consumed, so the point is moot. If the microalgae feeds shrimp larvae directly, that is only an added benefit.

As the shrimp larvae mature, the types of food combinations I give them change as well. The second and third weeks have newly-hatched Brine shrimp as the mainstay of the diet — being fed in the morning and late evening — with additions of powdered flake or freeze-dried foods in between. I alternate which inert foods they get at each feeding, relying on the concept that variety will supply them with whichever nutrients they require. The newly-hatched Brine shrimp circulate within the tank for hours, providing a constant supply of food items between varied, nonliving food servings.

By the fourth week, I begin adding some older Brine shrimp to the mix. Cleaner shrimp larvae don't begin to take adult Brine shrimp until week 5. By then, they are beginning to take on a stockier, more "shrimp-like" build. By week 6, they have functional pleopods, which they flutter on occasion. They also begin the "helicoptering" behaviors (where they grab onto the tank walls while still paddling their swimming legs furiously) that Peppermint shrimp larvae perform when they are getting ready to settle and become postlarvae.

The only thing they *don't* do is metamorphose. Phooey.

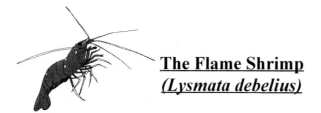

The Flame Shrimp
(Lysmata debelius)

The Flame shrimp, *Lysmata debelius*, are perhaps the prettiest shrimp I have ever seen. Deep wine red with white polka dots and bobby socks and white antennae, wow! (Only one deepwater shrimp has wowed me more. It had a pale pink, iridescent body with bold red and white stripes, and it walked on stilts. We brought a few of them up in a trawl from a research ship. As I turned the shrimp this way and that under the lights, observing its shimmering rainbows, I decided that one day I want to try working with those shrimp! Way cool!)

Flame shrimp also cost a lot, too. So of course, with my success with the Peppermint shrimp, I thought, oh boy, I'm gonna get rich! Oh what a jolly laugh I can imagine coming from aquaculturists everywhere.

The larvae are similar to Peppermint shrimp in all ways except color (they wear pink tuxedos and boxing gloves). They behave the same as Peppermint shrimp larvae in that they prefer to grab large objects. So you can feed them newly-hatched Brine shrimp or flake food (and more than one larva will share one flake). They are pretty hardy and they survive well — with the same care you give Peppermint shrimp larvae — until the fourth week. Then the mortalities begin. One by one, they drop off. I've had single larvae survive up to ten weeks and grow to an inch long from antenna-tip to spear-leg tip. At ten weeks, they are red with white legs and antennae, they are very stocky with easily seen pleopods and everything. They look so much like shrimp, that I'm just positive they'll settle to the bottom, but they never have (for me).

There is a place in England that made an announcement in Freshwater and Marine Aquarium Magazine telling the world that they succeeded in getting juvenile Flame shrimp — in apparently high numbers — but of course they wouldn't say how they did it. They reported that it took up to sixteen weeks for the larvae to settle, so perhaps it was some problem with the water quality in my larvae tanks, rather than some mysterious chemical or physical cue that the larvae were searching for.

Texas A & M University has also succeeded in bringing Flame shrimp through to metamorphosis. The Texas group contained their larvae in floating units similar to downwellers used in oyster and clam culture. These floating, screened containers were housed in very large fiberglass tanks that had regular filtration and frequent water exchanges. It also took approximately 16 weeks to get postlarvae. It may be that the larval cycle is just that long for Flame shrimp.

So, in the cases of both the Striped Cleaner shrimp and the Flame shrimp, call it an existence theorem. It is possible because it has been done. Just not by me.

Dern it.

Except for the actual settlement process, raising the larvae of Flame shrimp isn't too much of a problem, once you get the hang of it, that is. It's the adult shrimp that are the real problem. You might learn expensive lessons with these shrimp. A well-fed, healthy adult is fairly hardy. But don't count on your local store to keep them well-fed and healthy. While most marine aquarium stores have caring people who feed their animals the moment they settle into their tanks, there are still quite a few that don't bother. Many wholesalers are in the business of shipping in and shipping out aquatic animals as quickly as possible. It is considered time-consuming, water polluting, and uneconomical to feed the creatures in their care. The faster they can get it into a pet store, the less starvation it will face. However, if the aquarium store also is unethical and profit-minded, they too will attempt to skip feeding their animals and just try to sell them as quickly as possible before they eat each other or starve to death. What you usually get from those stores is a gorgeous, seemingly healthy, highly stressed and extremely fragile shrimp. You cannot tell if a shrimp is starving because its shell hides its suffering. It will look fine until the day it dies.

If you buy one of these starved animals, you will have to take extra precautions to prevent a quick death from overexertion. You should make their ride home as gentle and dark as possible to keep them from scrambling around their bag in panic. Also, their abilities to osmoregulate, or adjust to changes in salinity, will be compromised, so placing them into your tank may be quite time-consuming. It's best to recognize bad store management and refuse to buy these animals... even if they are the only ones in town that stock them.

If you shop at a quality aquarium store, then they usually ensure that their animals get fed well and housed in nonstressful conditions. Acclimating well-fed Flame shrimp to your home aquarium will still be more time-consuming than for "normal" shrimp, as these are fragile shrimp, but at least it won't be such a life-or-death delicate process.

I am happy to report that the number of "cheaper" aquarium suppliers appears to be dwindling due to educated consumers who ask, "has it eaten yet?" and even ask to be shown that it eats before purchasing the critter. All it takes is one bad experience to teach you to avoid buying cheaper stock. All of this adds to my reasons for wanting to captive-raise aquarium animals. Aquacultured fish and invertebrates are already adapted to aquarium conditions, so they will not experience the same stresses as wild-caught animals. They will be well-fed and healthy on arrival as they would be shipped directly to the store or supplier from the farm, and probably would not have to travel on long international flights... but let me get off my soap box now.

When introducing the shrimp to your aquarium, take your time. Sudden temperature or salinity changes, no matter how slight, can get the shrimp to freeze up in shock and die. They aren't quite that fragile later, after they are well-adjusted, but they are still pretty sensitive to salinity changes.

I usually float the bag in the tank, and over a period of two *hours*, I very gradually add tank water to the bag. You may get away with doing things faster, but I'm a poor child and would rather take my time than lose my money. I only mention this procedure because I *have* lost many shrimp due to the simple process of buying them and putting them into my aquarium.

Getting a pair is the next challenge. They are beautiful, but oh boy, are they aggressive with each other! The established one will chase a newly-introduced shrimp around and around the tank until it becomes exhausted. Then it becomes an expensive gourmet meal for the conquering shrimp. So you need to drastically alter the surroundings when introducing a new shrimp to the tank. Move some rocks, add new rocks, anything to distract the original shrimp. If you're adding two shrimp at once, then just make sure there are plenty of hidey-holes, and enough rocks so they can't see each other when they are at opposite ends of the tank.

Still, if one shrimp is significantly larger than the other — it doesn't matter if it's the established one or the new arrival — the larger one will chase the smaller one to death. Now, I tried this in 20 gallon tanks. Maybe in something larger, like a 55 gallon tank where they could spread out, they'd be okay. Somehow I doubt it. Right now there's a shrimp in Hawaii contemplating how it can chase and kill all the smaller shrimp off Africa. By the way, they only attack their own kind. You can have other species of *Lysmata* in the 20 gallon tank with them and they will generally ignore them.

So anyway, both Flame shrimp should be about the same size so that one won't get the "upper hand" over the other. They will tussle for a minute, until they both realize they've met their match, and then they'll pair up. It's kind of like a Klingon relationship (for those of you who never watch Star Trek, that means that each member of the pair has to be tough enough to take punch once in a while. If one wimps out, he or she is dinner). They might snip each other's antennae short on occasion, but otherwise they get along fine. And then you may have two and only two Flame shrimp in the tank or mayhem will occur.

The pair will get along with other shrimp species. You may have Peppermint shrimp and/or a pair of Cleaner shrimp in the same aquarium with them without problems. The Flame shrimp pair will be more secretive than the others, but they will also be the dominant ones come dinner time. They will eat first while the others back away.

Once established, they must not be disturbed. Just feed them, and then, before too long they will produce huge loads of orange eggs — which you may never see because the shrimp hide deep in shadowy crevices, and when they do come out, their thick red shells aren't transparent enough to view the eggs. The best thing to do is teach them to eat from your hand, which takes a *huge* amount of patience, because they are very skittish around giant hands.

On the night of hatching the eggs swell up so the "female" (both shrimp in the pair will produce fertile eggs) can't hide them from you anymore. Flame shrimp are more prone than any of the other kinds of shrimp to aborting the hatch and molting if you try to move a gravid shrimp into a larvae tank to hatch her eggs. You should definitely let the eggs hatch in the adult's aquarium and just collect the larvae.

The same dietary observations that I made with Striped Cleaner shrimp apply to Flame shrimp as well. Feeding the adults a diet high in carotenoid proteins creates active, feisty larvae that hatch with bold red colors. The larvae seem to have better survival until they reach 5-6 weeks old. Then, as with the Cleaner shrimp larvae, they slowly die out one by one, as if they are waiting for the appropriate signal that never arrives. By 10-12 weeks of age, I often only have a single survivor who eventually disappears.

Again, if you should happen to figure out what it takes to successfully grow these shrimp from egg to adult, please write me a letter or send me an email. I gotta know how close (or far away) I was to succeeding. If you don't want to tell me, then please, write to an aquarium magazine and tell the world. Don't keep it a secret.

The Coral Banded Shrimp
Stenopus hispidus

     I have only made a few trials with Coral Banded shrimp larvae (*Stenopus hispidus*), as I currently have no pair of my own. Some friends of mine owned a pair of Banded shrimp in their reef tank and allowed me to experiment with the adults and collect the larvae.

     As to obtaining a pair, Coral Banded shrimp are often sold as a pair. This is because they are monogamous and they do not switch genders as the shrimp in the genus *Lysmata* do. They remain either male or female all their life. How strange.

     Once "married" they will chase off and/or kill any others of their own species within reach. They are highly aggressive with their own kind, so you cannot have more than a single pair in an aquarium unless it is huge. Each pair expects to hold a territory of about 2 feet in diameter. If your aquarium is shorter than 3 feet long, that means you may have only 1 pair of Coral Banded shrimp in it. They get along fine with other shrimp species as long as everybody is well fed.

     The female Banded shrimp is usually the larger of the two. The male often is only half the size of his big wife. The female ordinarily has a bit more color on her undercarriage as well. She will have slightly more of the purple area than the male has. The easiest distinguishing feature, however, is when the female produces and lays her eggs. The eggs are teal or turquoise-colored, and you can view them while they are still in her ovaries. Shrimp ovaries lie on top and slightly aft of the other organs in what most people call the "head" of the shrimp (the carapace or cephalothorax area). If she is *very* ripe, the lengthening ovaries will extend into the uppermost "tail" area (technically the abdomen).

     When she lays her eggs and attaches them to her pleopods, the bluish area seems to disappear from her head and appear under her tail. The movement is a mystery to some folks. When you tell them they have been witnessing egg development and deposition, they seem so astonished. Sometimes they do not believe that shrimp lay or hold eggs, other times they seem amazed that you can see through a shrimp to its private parts.

The male fertilizes the female soon after she molts. The action usually occurs late at night when all is dark and private. In fact, this information is somewhat useful, as it can help you to create a new pair when necessary.

If one of the pair should happen to die, you can often re-pair the survivor if you follow these steps:
1) Be absolutely positive of the gender of both potential "mates".
2) Allow at least one molt cycle separation from the time of the first partner's death to the introduction of the new partner. That means that the surviving female shrimp should molt at least once after the death of her spouse, before meeting her new potential mate. If you have a male as a survivor, and you will introducing a new female, then just continue reading.
3) Make sure both shrimp are well-fed before the first date.
4) House the new potential partner in the same aquarium as the widow/widower, but keep the new shrimp confined in a screened container or plastic jar with holes all over it. This allows the male and female to smell each other without getting into fisticuffs. Float or anchor him/her near the widow/widower, making sure that there is enough water circulation to keep him/her from smothering in the container. The potential partner can remain in this container for weeks, if necessary, until the female molts. Of course, do not forget to feed the jailed shrimp.
5) Introduce the two immediately after the female molts. Observe them carefully throughout the day. The male may lose a claw to the female before she accepts him — that is fairly normal — but if he is starting to look battered (missing both claws and maybe his antennae and/or some legs), separate them again and try again another time. Or re-read step #1.

Egg development is similar to that described for Peppermint shrimp. The eggs gradually change from the original bright blue-green color of the first day, to grayish, then eventually to a highly reflective silver color. A flashlight will help to show you the reflective silver eyes of the larval shrimp within the eggs. On the night of hatching, the female often refuses food and her eggs begin to swell with water until the egg mass looks huge. Generally, Banded shrimp eggs take about 10 days to 2 weeks to hatch, depending on water temperature.

The larvae are very different from Peppermint shrimp larvae. For starters, they swim forward, in the direction of their eyes, rather than backwards as Peppermint shrimp larvae do. They still sort of orient themselves in a head down position, but they also swim horizontally. They are a little less than 2 mm long at hatching, and, for those of you who are familiar with commercial shrimp aquaculture, they look a bit like the mysis stage of Penaeid shrimp (the shrimp usually eaten at restaurants).

Newly hatched Coral Banded shrimp larvae will accept newly-hatched Brine shrimp as a first food, but they do not survive long with that as the sole food. Under the microscope, Coral Banded shrimp have bristly little legs that seem more adept at filter feeding, or grabbing much smaller prey like rotifers. Since they have been observed grabbing newly-hatched Brine shrimp, it means they will take "meat", but the basket-like fuzzy legs also might mean that they feed on microalgae as well.

The best survival I had with Coral Banded shrimp larvae was when I raised them similar to the way you might raise commercial Penaeid shrimp larvae. I used a large garbage can with a single airstone for gentle circulation. I added live microalgae (also known as greenwater) and rotifers, and then added the Banded shrimp larvae. I monitored the garbage can water color twice daily and added enough microalgae to barely cloud the water. By that I mean you should take a sample of water in a clear glass container, such as a beaker, and look through it with the light behind it. If it is clear, you need to add more microalgae. If it has a slight "fog" to it, then there is enough microalgae to feed the rotifers and/or shrimp larvae. I only added rotifers once per day during the first four days.

After the first 4 days, I began adding newly-hatched Brine shrimp to the mix. This went along fine for 2 weeks. The Coral Banded shrimp larvae molted, grew, and developed stalked eyes and more appendages.

The garbage can/Larvae Container was located in an outdoor area where it could get morning and late afternoon sunlight, but had a tarp for shade during the hottest part of the day. One day that tarp blew off, exposing the larval container to excessive Florida summertime heat. By the time I discovered the problem, it was too late. Everything except the Brine shrimp had been cooked.

I no longer have an outdoor area to work in, so I have not been able to recreate that trial. Attempting to do something similar indoors in 20 gallon glass aquaria has not been successful. The only reasons I can think of for why it worked so well outdoors, but has not worked indoors are:

1) The water volume of the garbage can contributed to a more stable water quality and/or the shape of the container made a more favorable water circulation.

2) Perhaps the early morning and late afternoon sunshine contributed some beneficial UV rays that broke down organics or kept disease organisms in check.

3) Some other unknown factor.

I have not done more trials with Banded shrimp larvae as I did not own the pair of Banded shrimp that contributed their larvae. My friends moved away, taking their shrimp pair with them. I know from reading various research papers that people have succeeded in raising Banded shrimp larvae through to metamorphosis. The methods that proved most successful were the ones where they reared them like — and, in fact, along with — commercial Penaeid shrimp larvae. The numbers that survived to metamorphosis were low, however, which leaves plenty of room for perfecting the process. Banded shrimp larvae either cannot compete with Penaeid shrimp larvae for access to enough food, or perhaps they require some other conditions to increase their settlement numbers.

Blue-Legged Hermit Crab
(Clibanarius tricolor)

Okay, it's a shrimp book, so what am I doing putting hermit crab information in this section? Well, I always keep some hermit crabs as janitors in my aquariums. They get whatever itty-bitty pieces of food that are leftover after the adult shrimp battle over it. I don't pay them much attention, except to give them larger shells when they need them. It is a bit amusing to watch them scuffle over the new digs. As soon as one crab moves out of his/her shell for the new one, somebody else tries on the now empty shell for size. And on it goes, with crabs taking each other's shells out for test drives until finally everybody is satisfied.

Anyway, happy hermit crabs breed, and since most members of the janitorial services get overlooked, hermit crab sex often goes unnoticed. But when you are collecting newly-hatched shrimp larvae nightly, you're bound to notice some occasional "extra" larvae if you have other species in the tank. So, since I'm reporting on other species here, I'll also report on the very few hermit crab larvae that I have raised along with my Peppermint shrimp larvae.

As to the conditions necessary for the hermit crabs to spawn, I did nothing special for them. All the conditions previously described for the Peppermint shrimp are what these hermit crabs experienced. I had a small colony of perhaps a dozen or so, and they got no different treatment. Even the food they received was merely hand-me-downs from the Peppermint shrimp.

The hermit crab larvae are approximately 2mm long at hatching, reddish in color, and look and swim vaguely like the previously described Coral Banded shrimp larvae. They orient themselves head down, but they swim forward, not backwards as Peppermint shrimp larvae do. Or sometimes they reverse course. But they always maintain the head down orientation.

Initially, they do not seem to feed on anything, or at least nothing that I have witnessed. It is possible that they feed on very microscopic food such as bacteria or microalgae. If I were ever to do a serious trial with hermit crab larvae, I might feed them rotifers and microalgae as the first foods. They will take newly-hatched Brine shrimp after 2 days or so, and a single newly-hatched Brine shrimp will keep a hermit crab larva busy for almost a whole day. They will also hold and eat finely powdered flake foods.

Again I did nothing special for the hermit crab larvae, as my main interest was in raising the Peppermint shrimp larvae, and a few hermit crab larvae survived to 4 weeks. At 4 weeks of age, they are approximately 4-5 mm in size and they swim and hunt newly-hatched Brine shrimp fairly well. They also begin to "touch down" on the bottom or sides of the aquarium and run along it with their tiny feet before lifting off and swimming away again. I never saw one metamorphose. I do not know if they require minuscule shells, or if they require some other food or chemical signals in order to trigger transformation into the first crab stage.

I realize that this is very sketchy information, but for those of you willing to give them a try, Blue-Legged Hermit crabs seem quite easy to breed and the larvae seem relatively hardy. If someone were to make a more serious effort, I believe these tiny janitors could be raised in serious numbers. As these Blue-Legged Hermit crabs are often found in areas dominated by Battalaria snails (whose shells they confiscate and inhabit), perhaps placing a few snails in their larvae tank at around 4 weeks of age would hasten their settlement and metamorphosis.

"Reef Lobster" (*Enoplometopus* sp.)

There are several species of "Reef Lobsters" available at aquarium stores. I am going to lump them all together here as their biology and behaviors are quite similar. Since I worked with them for a *very* short period of time, I will include what little I discovered here — in a shrimp book — in case anyone else would like to try their hand at breeding and raising these guys.

Reef Lobsters are not true lobsters, but are actually "lobster-like shrimp", which is the main reason they are included in this shrimp book. Reef Lobsters look vaguely like colorful, marine versions of freshwater crayfish or itty-bitty Maine (also known as North American) lobsters. They are quite beautiful, but they are exceedingly shy in an aquarium. They prefer deep, dark crevices, or they will create their own burrows underneath big rocks... which means that occasionally those big rocks will shift or tumble after enough sand has been excavated out from underneath them. Be warned.

Reef Lobsters come out of hiding mainly at night, although occasionally you'll spot them when they dart out and back quickly at feeding time. They grow to about 6 inches in length, but can begin reproducing at smaller sizes. Most of the ones you see in aquarium stores are approximately 2 inches long, which means they are still immature. You will probably have to get a pair of immature Reef Lobsters and wait until they are old enough to reproduce.

The two main species I attempted to culture were *Enoplometopus debelius*, also known as the Purple Reef Lobster for its vibrant purple color, and an unidentified species of *Enoplometopus*, possibly *E. antillensis* or *occidentalis*, sometimes called the Red Reef Lobster, probably due to its orange-red color. One other unidentified speckled specimen that I obtained remained a bachelor as I could never locate a mate for him.

I only succeeded in getting one pair of Purple Reef Lobsters to mate and produce eggs during the short experimentation period, which means that the information here may be limited... but it's a *lot* more than you'll find elsewhere.

The first and most difficult part is obtaining a pair. This is difficult for two main reasons:

1) They are quite rare, at least in aquarium stores. Even when you specifically order them, it may take a while before they arrive in the store, and it may take even longer to obtain two of the same species and opposite sex.

2) You have to get the permission of the aquarium store owner to hold the little lobster belly-side-up against the aquarium glass to determine

its gender before you buy it. This will garner many strange looks and questions, or simply a flat-out, "No. Buy it or don't". If you are willing and able, of course, you can buy up any you find and simply check their genders later, but I never had that much money to throw around.

As you may have deduced by the preceding paragraph, these Reef Lobsters have one gender all their lives. They are either male or female. Telling one from the other gets easier as they grow — meaning that it might be quite difficult to determine the gender of young individuals.

Like crayfish and Maine lobsters, the first pair of pleopods behind the walking legs of male Reef Lobsters have hardened into sperm delivery tubes called *petasma*. The average human might understand these devices better if you called them a pair of primitive penises. Crustaceans that have these sperm delivery devices generally have internal fertilization. The male must wait until the female has molted, and is soft and weak. Then he either flips her over or stands her up vertically and shoves these stiff tubes up close to or into the appropriate orifice.

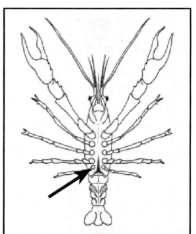

The first pair of pleopods in males are modified into sperm delivery tubes called petasma (arrow).

The petasmas, when not in use, usually are held flat against the underside of the carapace between the last two walking legs, and are sometimes hard to view unless you brush back the pleopods... then they stand up and get noticed. Well, you might need a magnifying glass. For practice, ask to see the undersides of Maine lobsters in your local market or seafood restaurant. It will be easier to tell males from females on those large creatures, so at least you will have an idea of what to look for on the smaller versions. It also adds a few minutes of interesting conversation to that boring dinner date.

Females have a pair of *gonopores* at the bases of their third walking legs. These tiny pores are where the eggs come out when the female lays them. When viewing a Reef Lobster upside down (or gently pressed, belly-up, against the aquarium glass) you might be able to see the two tiny spots at the base of the third pair of walking legs that give them a slightly more bulky appearance when compared to the other legs. To determine which are the third pair of walking legs, start counting from the back. The rearmost pair of walking legs are the fifth pair, the pair just forward of them would be the fourth pair of walking legs, the next ones up will be the third pair. But really, the males are a bit easier to identify. Ultimately, you determine the gender of Reef Lobsters in a kind of pass-fail manner: male or non-male.

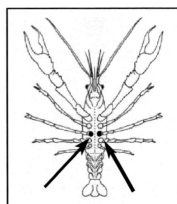

Females have 2 tiny gonopores at the base of the third pair of walking legs. The dots are exaggerated here to show location.

In the wild, Reef Lobsters tend to be solitary. They avoid their own kind. In an aquarium, they are territorial, and will rip the claws and legs off of any intruder, male or female. Luckily, their territories tend to be fairly small, and as long as they are happy in their burrows and well-fed, you can have more than one Reef Lobster in a tank as long as there is at least 12 inches of bottom space between them. More room is always safer.

My Reef Lobsters were kept as pairs in 10 gallon aquariums, with a screen divider down in the middle. They had both PVC pipes and rocks as hidey-holes. Most preferred the PVC pipes, especially if the pipes were half buried in the gravel so they had something to excavate.

And they lived like that for several months while they molted and grew and rearranged their homes. The males grew faster than the females. When they had reached approximately 4 inches long, I began to introduce them to each other, with supervision, to see how and when pairing occurred.

Every time the female molted, I would remove the divider and allow the two to meet each other. Often, the male would lunge out of his pipe the moment he realized something had changed in his territory. He would rush to attack or chase the intruder away. Then I would replace the divider after the female had lost some body part or another in the ensuing skirmish.

After a few tries like that with several pairs, I had almost decided that either I needed to rethink my match-making strategy, or that some other romantic factor might be missing.

Then, on the seventh attempt, the male Purple Reef Lobster lunged at the newly-molted female... and stopped. He pawed her gently for a bit with his claws, and then backed into his pipe with the female following. They spent the rest of the day together with the male guarding the entrance to the pipe. I have no idea what went on inside the pipe, as there seemed to be absolutely no activity after they entered.

By the next morning, the female was outside the pipe again, climbing as high up some rocks as she could without leaving the tank. She was missing a claw (again). The male brandished it in one of his, as if it were a trophy. The male wasn't after her at that moment, but it seemed clear that she wanted to leave, so I replaced the barrier and she seemed relieved.

The very next day, during a feeding, I noticed that she had eggs. Since the female was extremely secretive after the mating, only rarely could I observe her eggs during incubation. They did change colors over 2 weeks and began to develop eyes... but I missed the night of hatching. I never got another chance at duplicating the experiment due to a disaster that killed everything in the lab (mentioned in the chapter on commercial rearing).

As to the circumstances that led to the successful male and female coupling for a day, I can only guess at a few possibilities:
1) They both had finally matured enough to allow a reproductive attempt.
2) I had tried to remove the barrier as soon as possible in the morning after her molts, but perhaps my timing was better on the successful

mating day.

3) A cold front had moved through the area just a week before the successful mating. Here in sunny Florida, that means that the aquarium temperatures — which had no heaters to stabilize the temperatures — dropped to 70-72 F for several days before gradually warming back up to 79-80 F.

So, that's all the information I can add at this time. I hope it helps you, meager as it is. If you have any accomplishments at all, even if only a successful hatching, I would be pleased to know of it. As before, send me an email or write me a letter telling me of your achievements, or, if you don't want to tell me, then please write an article for an aquarium journal and tell everybody.

A Note on Commercial Rearing

I started raising Peppermint shrimp in my bedroom while I was still in High school. For two years, it was a hobby that slowly became an obsession. I did not want to give up until I'd succeeded in actually raising at least one danged little shrimp. I'm stubborn that way. If I feel like something's going to fail early on, before I've tried hard, then I have no problem with dropping it and moving on to something else. I can walk away and never give it a second thought. But if I think that something *is* possible, then I can't let it go even after running into one problem after another (or maybe *especially* after running into one problem after another). After I'd already invested a bunch of time and effort into the project, I wasn't gonna be defeated by some stupid little invertebrate that lacked a proper brain. That stubbornness set in and that's when my shrimp-raising hobby became less of a hobby and more of an obsession.

In a way, Peppermint shrimp helped me get through college. When a guidance counselor asked me what my hobbies were and I told her "raising shrimp", she said, "Oh, have I got a professor for you to meet", and about two weeks later I landed a job in a Crustacean Biology Lab. I learned loads there, while taking care of the University's Aquarium Room (among the things I learned in that Biology Lab was that you *do* occasionally use some of that drivel they cram into your head during classes). And the whole time I worked with shrimp and lobsters and crabs at school, I went home and "relaxed" with my home shrimp project.

I finally succeeded in bringing two Peppermint shrimp all the way through the larval cycle during my second year at college, but I didn't feel like dropping the project then. I wanted to see if it was possible to raise a bunch more. I started getting the hang of things and soon produced many more little shrimp which went to friends and a few aquarium stores.

Years later, I had time, I had a place (my mother's garage and spare bathroom), I had just recently gained experience growing large numbers of Redfish in a multi-tank system as part of a restocking effort in Miami, Florida, and, most important of all, I had encouragement from my mother and my husband, so I launched *Crunchy Critters*, an aquaculture venture that specialized in captive-raised invertebrates. In a 20' by 10' garage I housed a 700 gallon system to raise three species of shrimp in large numbers. Peppermint shrimp were to be the bread-n-butter while I experimented with the two relatives, *L. amboinensis* and *L. debelius.*

I was immediately socked with several problems I had never faced while the project had been a hobby. First, I discovered a fungus that attacked the shrimp eggs so that they only survived one week into the incubation before they turned white and died. The "female" kept holding the eggs, fanning and cleaning them like nothing was wrong, until the next week when she molted and discarded them. In the meantime, my supply of larvae dwindled while I tried to figure out what was going on (all the while cursing and kicking myself for bypassing quarantine procedures when introducing new broodstock to the system). Since Peppermint shrimp take about sixteen weeks to go from hatching to a marketable size, then the longer the delay between hatches, the longer your customers will have to wait for new shrimp (and the further away your paycheck gets).

The fungus that attacked my shrimp eggs was tentatively identified as *Lagenidium,* but treating for that disease didn't work out well. What finally solved the problem was to crash the entire broodstock (spawning tank) system. I removed the shrimp, put chlorine in the tanks and sump for 24 hours and then washed everything thoroughly. So basically, after my initial launch of a commercial aquaculture venture, I almost immediately flushed it and started over.

An aquaculture operation is a bit like a freight train. It takes a lot of time and effort to get it rolling, and if you stop it or de-rail it, it takes a while to get it moving again. So it's usually best not to totally disrupt your operation if you can help it. Crashing the system like that is a radical, last resort sort of measure. Sure, you may get rid of any disease organisms, but you also trash your biological filter/ecosystem, which takes a while to re-establish. The shrimp don't appreciate the disruption to their lives either and they quit producing eggs until after things have settled down for a while. Think about a major disaster like a hurricane or an earthquake. How long would it take *you* to return to normal behavior?

Anyway, I sterilized the tanks, restarted the system, put my shrimp back in and fed them well, and several weeks later, my adult shrimp began producing healthy eggs and larvae again.

Everything went along fine for a while, then suddenly the larvae began dying off in large numbers. They'd survive just fine, everything seeming normal, and then overnight I'd lose maybe 50%, and every night after that I'd lose the same amount until there were no more left to lose. Hooking up a UV sterilizer onto the larvae water supply solved that mysterious problem. I never identified it.

The next, and most disastrous, problem came when I began having difficulties getting enough Brine shrimp to hatch to feed my larvae. Tons of larvae starved. Once I discovered that the problem wasn't me or a certain can of Brine shrimp eggs, but that many people in the field of aquaculture were having the same problem, I felt a little better. Misery loves company.

I tried culturing other organisms to use as larval food. I experimented with copepods, but they reproduce too slowly to keep up with the demand, and their populations crash just when you really need them. I tried using mosquito larvae, since there were plenty of those in the backyard, but even though they survive surprisingly well in saltwater (around four hours, sometimes longer), they hang out motionless at the water surface, which does nothing to attract shrimp larvae. The shrimp larvae would grab and eat them if you stood around the tank and tapped each mosquito larva in turn to make it wriggle downwards, but golly, that's tedious.

I've already mentioned the trials with commercial shrimp feeds. I took a while to finally try flake food on the little buggers. Flake food was a wonderful discovery. Cheap, easy to store, nutritious, and the shrimp larvae actually ate it! It was time-consuming to feed, clean the tanks, and feed again, but it worked to bring Peppermint shrimp through metamorphosis. By eventually combining flake food feedings with a few wimpy Brine shrimp hatches, things worked out pretty well.

After those three major problems had been worked through, the business began to take shape. I started producing a dependable supply of shrimp, and I was beginning to sell them on a regular basis. It made me hope that this shrimp stuff might actually work out as a business. Then I started spending less time with the shrimp as I gave more time to my aging grandparents. Aquatic systems only allow you to do that for so long, and then all sorts of minor problems sneak up on you while you're not paying close attention. Filters clog, pumps fail, tanks overflow — or don't get any flow at all. All sorts of headaches. If you should try to raise any aquatic critter commercially, make sure you have plenty of time to devote to it, or it will definitely fail. Eventually I made a stupid mistake that killed off every one of my shrimp from larvae to adults. Crunchy Critters is yet another failed aquaculture statistic.

Even when things were going well, I discovered one other thing. Peppermint shrimp will not make you rich. You might be able to make the business pay for itself, but there won't be any take-home pay. Even when you produce large numbers of Peppermint shrimp, the cost of raising them is just about the same amount as the wholesale prices at the aquarium store. And egads, forget about selling your babies to the wholesalers themselves. They could only offer maybe half (if that) of what it cost to raise the shrimp. When people can get them cheaper from the wild, why should they pay more for captive-raised shrimp? So you more or less break even if you can sell directly to the aquarium stores. Flame shrimp or Striped Cleaner shrimp have higher wholesale prices, so if you can raise them in large numbers, that might almost become a real job, with a paycheck and everything.

The majority of the expense of raising Peppermint shrimp lies in the long, delicate larval life. The larvae require so much care, and the job of raising them is so time-consuming and tedious, that your success at larval culture is what will make or break your business. If you spend four weeks raising a batch of Peppermint shrimp larvae and then lose them over a small mistake, well, that sets you back four weeks.

Other saltwater ornamental species such as clownfish, which are starting to be regularly raised on a commercial basis, go through their larval cycle in a matter of days, not weeks. There's a better chance of being a financially viable business. Raising fragile larvae is a bit like crossing a high wire. If the wire is a half mile long, there's more time to make a mistake than if it's only ten feet long.

If you do decide to try raising these shrimp commercially, obviously your system and techniques will have to change slightly from the hobbyist method. You will have to change your larvae tank arrangement and maintenance procedures slightly as daily, or even weekly, water changes to individual tanks becomes a huge time-consumer. You should devise some kind of a slow, constant water exchange for the larvae tanks, like a drip irrigation system that adds water into each tank, so that the entire volume of each larvae tank gets changed at least once per day. That will help keep the water quality stable, instead of degrading over time like it does when using the hobbyist method. I haven't found any alternative to the bottom siphoning procedures described earlier. You still need to get rid of the built-up detritus on the bottom of the tanks or the larvae will become entrapped in it and smother. That's tedious, but with practice you'll learn to judge just about how much food to feed your larvae so that there's a minimum of excess to fall to the bottom for you to clean up. I eventually got the timing down to five minutes per larvae tank on cleaning day.

You will also need plenty of broodstock shrimp (the adults) in order to produce the thousands of larvae which may eventually turn into hundreds of little shrimp. You will need a filtration system capable of handling the load. Frank Hoff's book, *Conditioning, Spawning, and Rearing of Fish with Emphasis on Marine Clownfish* describes various systems in detail, so I won't repeat all that here. There are many other helpful books and articles, so I'll just put some of them in the bibliography at the end of this book so you can read them for more information. A few of them even describe some of the problems and solutions of moving from an experimental system to a commercial system.

I would like to mention one more thing of importance when designing your system. You should design your system to prevent problems in case of electrical or mechanical failures, or human error. I had originally designed my system so that all the tanks — broodstock, larvae and growout — drained into the same sump. Maintaining the water quality to all those tanks was a breeze, and I never had to worry about salinity or temperature differences when moving animals from tank to tank. I had a UV sterilizer on the water supply lines to keep diseases under control, and I also had a separate air system for all the tanks in case the water supply should stop due to a pump failure. I also installed individual undergravel filters into each of the broodstock and growout tanks, again in case of a water pump failure that stopped the flow of new water into the tanks. I have found that air pumps are far more reliable than water pumps, so I always design them into the system as a backup to a sudden water pump failure.

The down side to having a communal water supply is that if you screw up, the entire system will be affected. If you, say, drip in freshwater from a hose to make up for evaporation and forget and leave it on all night, that will kill everything in the system from the shrimp to the beneficial bacteria in your filters. This is what happened to *Crunchy Critters*. In one moment of forgetfulness, a fledgling aquaculture operation went out of business.

If instead, your broodstock tanks, larvae tanks and growout tanks each have their own separate sumps and filters, then *when (not if)* you screw up, it might hurt, but at least you won't have affected everything. You have to devise ways to prevent human error, such as perhaps using a float valve to automatically shut off incoming water after it has reached the correct level, and other such ideas.

Someday I may try to revive *Crunchy Critters*. When I do, I'll redesign the system with all those previous mistakes in mind. I would also like to try to find a better way to more thoroughly circulate and filter the water in the individual larvae tanks. Even though the rate that water entered and exited the individual tanks was enough to theoretically empty and refill the tank (in the later larval stages) once every four hours, there may not have been a complete flushing. Larvae that took five weeks to become postlarvae and moved on to the growout tanks did well, whereas larvae that took longer than ten weeks to reach metamorphosis died. If the reason is not that they were waiting for some mysterious chemical cue, then it probably was a water quality problem — something that took over five weeks to become a hazard. A better water turnover won't harm anything, and it will help to eliminate that question from the larvae settlement problem.

So, good luck if you do try to raise ornamental shrimp commercially.

And don't forget to quarantine any new animals before putting them into your system.

Designing a Seriously-Committed Hobbyist System or Small-Scale Commercial System for Crustaceans

They're called aqua-nuts. Or fishophiles. Obsessed or deranged. They are the hobbyists who cannot stop at just one aquarium. Before long, anything that can hold water is viewed as a possible aquarium. If you begin to have luck breeding and raising shrimp, you might find yourself having to turn sideways to squeeze between aquariums and garbage cans and other containers filled with burbling water. Eventually, a spouse or a friend will encourage you to organize your hobby into its own space. And thus, the Fish Room is created.

The Fish Room can be merely a scaled up passion of an avid hobbyist, or it can be the initial stages of entrepreneurship. The previous chapter only skimmed the surface of commercial aquarium shrimp rearing. In this chapter I will try to be more specific. This discussion will describe a system that will be a fairly large step up from a couple of fun hobby tanks. And it will be a step down from a true commercial-scale business. I will begin with a discussion of the garage-sized system I originally designed, then I will offer suggestions for how to improve that system. My original system used 20 gallon aquaria for all operations, from broodstock housing, to larval rearing, to juvenile growout. So, unless otherwise specified, any time I use the words "tank" or "aquarium", I mean a 20 gallon-sized aquarium.

A garage, basement, or shed may be used to produce fair numbers of shrimp, and work out your personal difficulties before attempting to upscale to a full-time business. Selling a few shrimp directly to retailers or aquarists is possible as a side business from home. If it starts to become profitable, and you want to take the gamble, your next step up could be renting a warehouse, to allow more, and bigger, tanks.

Although I mentioned in the previous chapter that a common water system can be a recipe for a whole system disaster, there are pros and cons to a common sump. I still believe that the pros outweigh the cons, and suggest that you should simply design safeguards against forgetfulness, disease, clogged filters, and any other difficulties that could arise. Having multiple individual systems rather than a single combined water source means an easier time of isolating and solving problems, but it also means water quality will vary among the separate systems, however slightly. Larvae are quite sensitive to any changes, and although they might survive the stresses, it seems wrong to add an unnecessary stress of any kind. There will be more than enough without the additional transfer-and-acclimation stress. Having a single water system means saving time as well, because you do not have to acclimate the larvae to temperature or salinity variations when transferring them to their larval aquaria. You can just pick them up and gently pour them into their new homes. You can decide for yourself which is the better system for you. *Crunchy Critters* had a single sump for all of the broodstock, larval and growout tanks, so that's what I will be describing.

The broodstock tanks — the aquariums that house the adult pairs of shrimp — should be placed somewhere that does not get a lot of traffic so they will be disturbed as little as possible. In my garage space, that meant placing a row of broodstock aquaria against the farthest wall. The diagram on page 118 shows the basic layout of *Crunchy Critters.*

With Peppermint shrimp, you can keep small colonies of adults in 20 gallon tanks. My original system started with 5 broodstock tanks and total of 30 Peppermint shrimp. Certainly not a number that would impress true full-scale aquaculture operations, but with that number of adults, you will get multiple daily hatches of larvae to distribute to the larvae tanks. Later on, I added more broodstock tanks, and other species, as well.

I had dual filtration systems on the broodstock and growout tanks, as briefly mentioned in the previous chapter. They had air-driven undergravel filters in the tanks themselves, and there was a spraybar and overflow that exchanged aquarium water with the common sump (which had its own filtration). The reason for the dual filtration systems is that air pumps generally are more reliable, long term, than water pumps. Also, spraybars, no matter how you set them, always need readjusting, cleaning, unclogging, and/or sometimes they just decide to take an unscheduled vacation. It never fails that a power surge or some other fluctuation causes one tank or another to stop receiving a decent flow of water. And it never fails that that happens only at night, so it is always morning, several hours later, when you first discover the problem.

Having air-driven filtration and circulation means that in the event of a water supply failure, the inhabitants remain healthy. Another bonus, if you use automatic battery-backup air pumps to run the undergravel filters, is that you can virtually ignore power outages. On the extreme end, my current experimental shrimp breeding system survived 2 minor hurricanes that knocked out the power for 9 and 11 days each. Obviously, for power failures of that length of time, you will need to recharge or replace batteries on the air pumps, but at least it gets you through the first 24 hours before you have to get concerned.

As a side note, it does not take long for hydrogen sulfide gas to build up in dirty filters during a electrical failure. When the power comes back on and the water begins flowing through them again, that sludgy, smelly, poisonous water from the filters will circulate throughout your system. If you know that your power will be out for longer than 24 hours, you should begin cleaning and/or emptying out all of your stagnant filters as a precaution. And, hey, they probably needed it anyway. Another precaution would be to divert all of the water from the animal tanks and force the sump to recirculate itself for a couple of hours after the electricity is restored. Circulation and aeration is the enemy of hydrogen sulfide.

Next up is the need for a non-disturbing, non-time-consuming way to collect the larvae that hatch during the night. You can build and use the individual Larvae Collectors described in chapter 5, but positioning them nightly, cleaning them daily, plus the careful siphoning of the larvae the next morning gets tedious and time-consuming. Something non-invasive and passive, such as employing the already flowing water through the brood tanks to gently gather the larvae into a communal collection area, is ideal.

Rather than the broodstock water overflowing and crashing down through a series of pipes straight to the sump's prefilter, you need to alter the piping arrangements slightly, so that any water heading downward travels at a 45 degree (or less) angle to create a more gradual descent. If that seems like it is too hazardous for fragile larvae, remember that they are only 2mm long at hatching, and as long as they experience no sudden changes of direction or whitewater rapids, they are nothing but dust particles going with the flow. Think of it as a flume at a water theme park, slooshing the larvae gently to their collection area.

Just before the prefilter is a wide, easily accessible box, similar to a sediment filter, that slows the water flow greatly by spreading it out. A screen, designed to prevent larvae from escaping the box, stretches across the complete width of the box. The width of the box allows the speed of a large volume of water to slacken. The slower flow keeps the larvae from being crushed up against the screen as the water heads out to the sump. As the larval collector screen acts a bit like a pre-prefilter, it needs to be removable so it can be detached and cleaned every day, after the previous night's larvae have been harvested.

Then all you need is a dim light source that attracts the newly hatched larvae toward the broodstock tanks' outflowing water during the night. The larvae still need to be siphoned or scooped from the collection area into containers for transfer to the larval rearing tanks, but the process is made much smoother by the larvae being gathered all in one place.

The diagram on page 118 shows the basic floor plan for *Crunchy Critters*. An approximately 240 gallon communal sump was built underneath the broodstock tanks. It had a large prefilter where all the water returns from the broodstock, growout, and larvae tanks entered. From there the water entered the biological filter before passing through a large protein skimmer and chemical filtration areas. A single water pump, slightly more powerful than the whole system required, moved filtered water from the sump back to the broodstock, larvae, and growout tanks. Excess water returned to the sump's prefilter for re-filtration. If you are doing this as a serious business, rather than as an intense hobby/side job, then you would need a spare water pump ready to replace the main water pump whenever it required servicing.

The water heading to the larvae tanks requires extra filtration. Two cartridge filters in line on the larval water supply pipe — the first, a 20 micron cartridge and the second a 1 micron cartridge — clarifies the water and prevents possible pests from entering the larval tanks. No matter how careful you are, small predatory amphipods and/or other minute critters can occasionally survive passage through the regular filtration and colonize your larvae tanks if you don't have this microfiltration. These two filters, especially the 1 micron cartridge, will require frequent cleaning or replacement, to maintain good water flow to the larvae tanks.

The next filter in line after the microfiltration, the UV sterilizer, is the most important, as it prevents viruses, bacteria, fungi, and other non-filterable baddies from entering the larvae tanks. Make sure you size it correctly for your water flow to get the correct "kill" rate.

The larvae tanks had the same basic arrangement as described earlier in this book — each larvae tank was a bare bottomed, dark-sided, 20 gallon aquarium with a single airstone bubbling gently in the corner. The addition to this arrangement was a single stream of filtered saltwater which added to the slow circulation in the tank. The incoming water dribbled just enough to fill an empty aquarium in a day. As the larvae grow, you can increase the water flow a little.

This water addition was used mainly to balance the system and keep each tank at the same salinity and other water parameters as all the other tanks. I still had to siphon debris off the bottoms of the aquariums, although with the incoming water stabilizing the water quality I could limit the vacuuming chores to once per week.

The outflowing water had to have screens to prevent the larvae from escaping their tank and entering the main filtration system, and the screens required fairly large surface areas to prevent

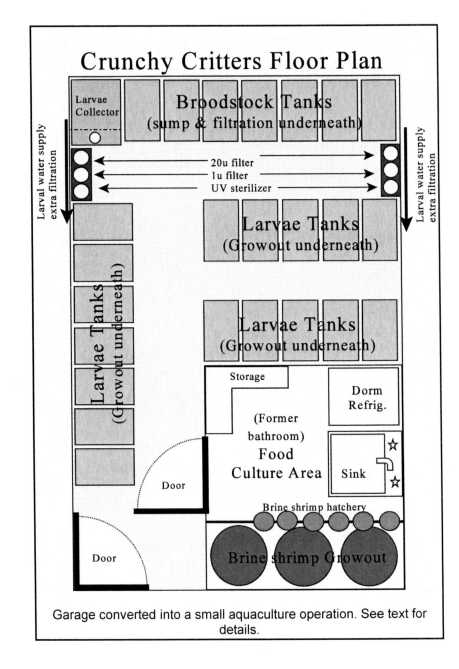

Garage converted into a small aquaculture operation. See text for details.

the larvae from getting sucked up onto them. For this I utilized the same 2 liter bottle idea as I did for the homemade Larvae Collector. I love those 2 liter soda bottles. I come up with all sorts of uses for them. They're cheap (or free, if you go dumpster-diving for them), easy to clean, and easy to cut and glue.

For the outflow screens, cut off the bottom of a plastic 2-liter soda bottle, leave the screw cap in place, and cut out large sections of the sides. It's best to create 3 or 4 large "windows" in the sides, so as to create a fairly rigid framework for the screens. Then, using hot glue or silicone, glue the screens in place. As before, be sure to seal all edges to prevent the larvae from escaping or getting tangled in raw screen material.

The last bit of construction is to drill 2 holes near the open end, in a similar arrangement to the brine shrimp hatchery described earlier in this book. Tie a string from one hole to the next, or create a wire loop that connects the two holes to create a hanger. A large dowel was suspended approximately 6 inches above the backs of the larvae tanks, with properly spaced nails to hang these outflow screens in the correct positions.

With multiple soda bottles ready with screens already glued in place, you can quickly exchange them as they clog up. The outflows for my individual larvae tanks were simple U-shaped siphon overflow tubes. It was a simple process to remove the siphon tube, change out a dirty outflow screen for a clean one, then replace and restart the siphon tubes. The entire procedure took less than a minute.

You can glue different mesh screens onto individual bottles, so that as the larvae grow, you can gradually change the screen mesh size to allow faster water flows and more debris removal. But really, it's not so much the larvae that you size the screens for, but rather their food. Too large a mesh and all those expensive newly-hatched Brine shrimp will wash out into the sump's prefilter and your shrimp larvae will starve until the next feeding. As the larvae's *food* grows, you can change screen sizes.

Using the slow water exchange system allows more shrimp larvae to metamorphose into postlarvae. Whether that is due to the increased circulation and/or aeration (as the incoming water entered as a tiny spray), or due to the more stabilized water quality, without the fluctuations of batch water changes, I am not sure.

After a few weeks of conditioning the adults, they began breeding and providing me with daily hatches of larvae. On average, I got about 300 larvae per day. Some days more, some days less. I rarely counted the larvae when stocking them (except when I began attempting to raise *Lysmata debelius*, the Flame shrimp). I already had a lot of practice raising Peppermint shrimp larvae as a hobby, so I could "eyeball" the appropriate population densities in the larvae tanks. Sometimes a single day's hatching would fill a larvae tank, sometimes a single day's hatching would take up 2 or more tanks, depending on how many spawns occurred on a given evening. Sometimes it would take 3 days to add enough shrimp larvae to a single aquarium. You can add newly hatched larvae to aquariums with slightly older larvae, like say, at most a week older. Any older than that, and you get too much of a size difference, which translates into a food size difference.

After 5-6 weeks, the larvae began metamorphosing, which took several days for all to complete the transition to a bottom-dwelling lifestyle. I often left the tiny shrimp to grow for another week in the larvae tank before transferring them to a Growout tank, which had basically the same arrangement as the adult Broodstock tanks, except the outflow had a finer screen on it to prevent escapes. The now-empty larvae tank was then thoroughly cleaned and sterilized (an important step) for the next batch of hatchlings.

And that was *Crunchy Critters* before its demise. If I were to do it all again, in the same garage-type setting, I might use separate water pumps for each section. The broodstock tanks would have their own water pump, the larvae tanks would have their own, etc. Reasons for this are mainly that adjusting the water flow to one tank meant some tank, somewhere else in the whole system, would end up with reduced or increased water flow... often not noticeable for an hour or more. It meant a lot of time wasted on: adjusting the water flow to a single tank, waiting about an hour, readjusting water flows to one or more affected tanks, waiting another hour, and so on.

Water goes wherever there is the least resistance. For example, while the larvae tanks themselves did not require much overall volume, increased pressure was needed for their microfiltration. And a reduction in pressure due to increasing some flow in, say, a broodstock tank, often resulted in a complete stoppage of water flow to one or all of the larvae tanks.

With individual water circulation, it would be easier to monitor and adjust water flows on the different sections. It would also mean that if a single water pump failed, its failure would not affect any of the other sections. And as a bonus, ordinarily you can buy several smaller pumps for the price of a single large pump. Ensure that if you do decide to use multiple smaller pumps, you choose pumps with more power than you require, so that you will be able to add more tanks to the system as time, space, and money allow, without having to upgrade the pump(s). Just return any "excess" water to the sump.

If, after you have stretched your legs, so to speak, with a home-based operation, you decide you'd like to try this shrimp raising stuff as a real business, then think these thoughts:

- When you move out of the house, your shrimp will have to be self-sufficient. They will now have to pay the rent and electricity, among other things that you take for granted at home.

- You will need "coasting money" — funds for the startup and operation costs of the business — that far exceed what's needed for a normal business. Aquaculture operations average 5 years before they break even... if they ever do. You will also need "emergency funds" for that crisis you did not think of. Banks and insurance companies are not suckers. Most will not cover aquaculture operations due to their history of frequently losing everything overnight. *Aquaculture is agriculture* is a slogan that Florida aquaculturists began in an effort to get equal farmer-style treatment from banks, insurance companies, and state legislators. But heh, heh, try it.

• Scaling up from a hobbyist system is not as simple as just increasing the number of tanks. You may need to redesign your system to accommodate more, and larger, tanks. You may need to rethink the routine cleaning and maintenance of those more cumbersome tanks. Will you need (and can you pay for) an employee? Where and how will you sell your shrimp? If you have been selling directly to aquarists or stores, can you seriously continue to do that on a larger scale? While still devoting enough time to the critical process of raising the shrimp? Or will you sell to the distributors... who will pay you a lot less per shrimp?

There is lot about scaling up an aquaculture operation that has been more thoroughly described in other books and journals, and you should probably consult those. See the *Suggested Reading* section for ideas on where to start. As this is a hobbyist book, let's go back to the hobby end of things.

You can still have a home-based system that brings in some side money, and, in some cases, pretty good money, so long as you aren't depending on the income, and your main job is absorbing the electricity, rent, and other costs. Other ways to increase the profits are to raise something rare or hard to get. You can use some of the ideas in this book to experiment with other aquatic critters that have not yet been raised in captivity and/or are difficult to find during their "off season". Or, occasionally, you can develop a demand for even the most "common"critters if you happen upon a new strain.

Freshwater fish that were successfully bred and raised repeatedly in captivity led to the development of longer fins, new or bolder colors, different body shapes, and more, simply because you are able to pick pairs with certain characteristics and breed them together. The modern freshwater captive-raised aquarium fish often bears little resemblance to its wild counterparts.

Clownfish have become the first marine fish to have several generations that have never seen the ocean. In doing so, there are already clownfish specimens available for sale that you would never see in the wild. Some have very black fins, or completely black bodies, or large portions of white, or round spots instead of stripes. Routine captive-breeding allows selection for unusual or preferred characteristics, which is the hallmark of domestication.

There is the opportunity to do something similar in shrimp, too. In Peppermint shrimp, I have noticed some individuals with no "clear areas" on their bodies. Normal, wild-type coloration of Peppermint shrimp is red stripes on a transparent background, resulting in an overall pale pinkish cast when seen from a distance. The occasional mutant Peppermint shrimp has red stripes on a translucent reddish background. This makes it stand out from a distance. "Super-Red" Peppermint shrimp could possibly command a slightly higher price if they are deemed marketable, as they would be both useful (by eating those pesky Aiptasia anemones) and more noticeable.

If you are going to try to breed for specific characteristics, then you may have to use smaller tanks, or divide the larger tanks into two or more smaller compartments in order to house specific pairs together. You would also need to return to using the in-tank Larval Collector device described in chapter 5 (or create your own version) to gather the larvae from these specific pairs, as combining those shrimp larvae with hundreds of others from miscellaneous breeding pairs defeats the purpose.

With a home-based side business, you would be able to experiment with animals and inventions that you could never do while attempting to run a profit-minded business. The burden of making ends meet limits serendipity. You could do more for both the hobby and the industry by tinkering in your Fish Room, and then reporting all that you find out. The occasional sale will merely feed your obsession.

So, support your local aqua-nut!

A Request

Well, parts of the last three chapters reminded me of a pet peeve of mine. In order to be economically viable in the aquaculture industry, you have to have a virtual monopoly of the market. The only way to keep that monopoly is to be close-mouthed about your techniques and latest discoveries. It costs a lot, in both time and money, to raise any aquatic species, especially saltwater ornamentals, so you want to be the only one doing it.

At first, back when I was a dumb ol' hobbyist who just wanted to raise ornamental shrimp for fun, that attitude really irritated me. I mean, I wasn't trying to compete, I was just a high school kid goofing around. I just wanted to learn. At the time I wasn't even working on a species of shrimp that anyone cared much about. It was a novelty. Since no one else had ever raised Peppermint shrimp before, or at least hadn't written anything about it, I had nothing to refer to. Most scientific research papers dealing with aquaculture were written about commercially valuable species such as food fish and shrimp. I found very little information on raising saltwater tropicals (except in hobbyist magazines).

While looking for information and guidance at various aquaculture facilities, I ran into walls of suspicion, as if I were some kind of corporate spy disguised as a High school student. Even the friendlier folks still gave me half-answers and hints instead of open, up-front elucidations.

I remember one marine aquarium society meeting where the guest speaker was someone who had commercially raised clownfish for a major aquarium salt manufacturer. I attended the meeting with hope that I might finally get some useful information for a change. About 70% of his answers, however, were, "that's proprietary information, I can't answer that" and I left that meeting disappointed and a little angry.

Later, after I had finally learned how to raise Peppermint shrimp — *on my own* — after I had fought so hard to find information, and after killing off literally thousands of larvae, I finally hit on the right combinations and raised some shrimp. It was a happy time... and it made me suddenly understand (sort of) why no one wanted to give out free information. There's this kind of selfish feeling that makes you want to say, "I'm not going to make it easy on you, struggle a little, like I had to". That selfish feeling also wars with another one. There's a kind of joy in spreading the news. Keeping secrets bothers the soul, I think.

When I made my commercial attempt, I feel like I did a pretty good job — up until the time that I killed off all my shrimp, I suppose — and I wanted to keep the techniques and other things I'd learned to myself, to give me that edge over the other two aquaculture enterprises that were just beginning to raise the same brands of shrimp. But now that I've had the time to think about it, I had a revelation. The only way to lower the costs associated with raising saltwater tropicals is to give the information to a bunch of different people. People with different educational backgrounds will try new, previously unthought-of ways to accomplish the same things. As evidenced by the ideas presented by hobbyists in the various aquarium magazines, there are many ways to do things and someone, somewhere, may invent some device or possibly develop some new technique that makes raising fish and invertebrate larvae simple and worry-free.

One day, the importation of fish and shrimp and corals may be banned, just like the importation of parrots and other species from South America and Australia have already been banned. Right now, the only (legal) way to have a parrot is to get a hand-raised one, hatched right here in North America from captive pairs. They don't (legally) capture them from the wild any more. The same thing may happen someday to the aquarium industry and then the only things that will be available to aquarium hobbyists will be whatever can be grown in captivity.

The happy news is that most aquarium hobbyists are more than willing to share the news of some new discovery or observation they've had. A lot of marine aquarium societies now have breeder's groups that get together to work out solutions to problems they have. There is also now a Breeder's Registry which allows people from all over to access information from other hobbyists nationwide. It's a great start, but the information there is always a little slim on details. The best, most detailed information for hobbyists comes from either aquarium magazine articles or books like this one.

As of 2007, there is also now a Project DIBS — which stands for Desirable Invertebrates Breeding Society. They are challenging aquarists to propagate various invertebrates in captivity. And they are encouraging them to breed and report on not just the pretty corals and shrimp, but also some of the "lowly" and forgotten aquarium inhabitants such as snails, hermit crabs, and other janitorial services members. This was what inspired me to include the few paragraphs on my few Blue-Legged Hermit crab spawns. Otherwise, I would never have thought that could be useful information to anybody. Check out the *References & Suggested Reading* section if you want to find out more about Project DIBS.

Even thirty years ago, there were some species of freshwater tropical fish that were believed to be impossible to raise in captivity, but the freshwater enthusiasts kept at it, sharing their information at meetings and in magazines and books (just look at all those specialty books written on just one kind of fish like guppies or bettas or *Corydoras* catfish). Now almost all the freshwater fish you see in aquarium stores are captive-raised. That's great.

I write this stuff here, giving away everything that I know, and telling as many experiences as I feel I can tell without boring people silly, so that others out there can have a little fun. And maybe while those people are amusing themselves, they might discover or invent something new along the way that suddenly revolutionizes the hobby (and the business). So, write articles, tell the world what you discover and don't skimp on the details. Our hobby may depend on it.

References and Suggested Reading

Some of these works were referred to in the text. The rest are just useful for learning more about aquaculture in general or crustaceans in particular.

Adey, Walter H. and Karen Loveland. 1991. **Dynamic Aquaria: Building Living Ecosystems.** Academic Press, Inc. San Diego, CA, USA. 643 pp.

Colin, Patrick L. and Colin Patrick I. 1989. **Marine Invertebrates and Plants of the Living Reef.** TFH Publications, Inc. Ltd. Neptune City, NJ. USA.

Hoff, F. H. 1996. **Conditioning, Spawning and Rearing of Fish With Emphasis on Marine Clownfish**. Aquaculture Consultants, Inc. Dade City, FL, USA. 212 pp.

Hoff, F. H. and T. W. Snell 1987. **Plankton Culture Manual**. Florida Aqua Farms, Inc. Dade City, FL, USA. 155 pp.

Landau, Matthew. 1991. **Introduction To Aquaculture.** John Wiley & Sons. USA.

McVey, James P. (editor). 1993. **CRC Handbook of Mariculture: Crustacean Aquaculture**. CRC Press. USA.

Moe, Martin A. Jr. 1997. **Breeding The Orchid Dottyback: An Aquarist's Journal.** Green Turtle Publications. Plantation, FL, USA. 285 pp.

Moe, Martin A. Jr. 1992. **The Marine Aquarium Handbook: Beginner To Breeder.** Green Turtle Publications. Plantation, FL, USA.

320 pp.

Moe, Martin A. Jr. 1991. **Lobsters: Florida, Bahamas, the Caribbean.** Green Turtle Publications. Plantation, FL, USA. 512 pp.

O'Connor, Nancy J. 1991. **Flexibility In Timing Of The Metamorphic Molt By Fiddler Crab Megalopae** *Uca pugilator.* Marine Ecology Progress Series. Volume 68: 243-247.

Riley, C. M. 1994. **Captive Spawning and Rearing of the Peppermint Shrimp** *(Lysmata wurdemanni).* Seascope. Volume 11, Summer issue. p. 4

Spotte, S. 1970. **Fish and Invertebrate Culture: Water Management in Closed Systems.** John Wiley & Sons. NY, USA. 145 pp.

Sweatman, Hugh. 1988. **Field Evidence That Settling Coral Reef Fish Larvae Detect Resident Fishes Using Dissolved Chemical Cues.** Journal of Experimental Marine Biology & Ecology. Volume 124: 163-174

Treece, Granvil D. and Joe M. Fox. 1993. **Design, Operation and Training Manual for an Intensive Culture Shrimp Hatchery.** Texas A&M University Sea Grant College Program, Galveston, TX, USA. 187 pp.

Wilkerson, J.D. 1994. **Scarlet Cleaner Shrimp: Care and Reproductive Habits of** *Lysmata amboinensis.* Freshwater and Marine Aquarium Magazine. Vol. 17.

Wilkerson, J.D. 1997. **Clownfish: A Guide To Their Captive Care, Breeding, and Natural History.** Microcosm Ltd., Shelburne, VT. USA. 216 pp.

Aquaculture Suppliers

This list has but a few of the many aquaculture suppliers that will at least talk to hobbyists. For a much longer list, check out Aquaculture Magazine's Buyers Guide (see magazine listing).

Aquacenter, Inc.
166 Seven Oaks Road, Leland, MS 38756
1-800-748-8921

Aquatic Ecosystems, Inc.
1767 Benbow Court, Apopka, FL 32703
(407) 886-3939

Carolina Biological Supply
2700 York Road, Burlington, NC 27215
1-800-334-5551

Florida Aqua Farms /Aquaculture Supply
33418 Old Saint Joe Road, Dade City, FL 33525
(352) 567-0226

Miami Aqua-culture, Inc. / Marine Scenes
805 North Federal Highway, Boynton Beach, FL 33435
(561) 364-5527

There are plenty of hobbyist and professional magazines that are very helpful, but I'll only mention a few of the more popular ones here. (Project DIBS, also mentioned below, isn't a magazine, but rather an online forum dedicated to the rearing of aquarium-related invertebrates.)

Aquaculture Magazine
P.O. Box 2329

Asheville, NC 28802

Aquarium Fish Magazine
P.O. Box 53351
Boulder, CO 80322-3351

Freshwater & Marine Aquarium Magazine
R/C Modeler Corp.
P.O. Box 487
Sierra Madre, CA 91024

Project DIBS
The Reef Stewardship Foundation
P.O. Box 84238
Pearland, TX 77584
www.projectdibs.com

SeaScope
Aquarium Systems, Inc.
8141 Tyler Blvd.
Mentor, OH 44060

The Breeder's Registry (Journal of Maquaculture)
P.O. Box 255373
Sacramento, CA 95865

Tropical Fish Hobbyist
TFH Publications, Inc.
One TFH Plaza
Neptune City, NJ 07753

Index

Stoichactis
        helianthus 86
Toxin 73,74,76
Uropods 8,9,29
Vacuum cleaner 44
Zinc 73
Zoea 28

About The Author

April Kirkendoll is a biologist, professional aquaculturist and marine aquarist who has worked with Peppermint shrimp for 24 years. In 1997 she started *Crunchy Critters*, an aquaculture venture that specialized in captive-raised invertebrates. She raised Peppermint shrimp in commercial numbers and experimented with two related species of cleaner shrimp and two species of reef lobsters.

She also has spent over 30 years studying cancer in order to more thoroughly understand this odd, highly variable disease. In 2004, she wrote *The End of Cancer: Seeking A New Understanding To Defeat the Enemy Within*, which summarizes and rethinks a century's worth of cancer data for nonscientists.

She lives in Florida with her husband and a whole menagerie of animals that functions as their kids.